Folly Cove Sketches

Remembering Virginia Lee Burton

June Vail

FOLLY COVE SKETCHES
Remembering Virginia Lee Burton
Copyright © 2022 June Vail

ISBN: 978-1-63381-305-2

Cover photograph: Virginia Lee Burton in Studio, ca. 1948. Photograph by Gerda Peterich. Image courtesy of the Cape Ann Museum Library & Archives, Gloucester, MA.

Cover artwork: Virginia Lee Demetrios (1909–1968), *Winter Boarders*, undated, ink on linen, linoleum block print. Collection of the Cape Ann Museum, Gloucester, MA.

Designed and produced by
Custom Museum Publishing
12 High Street, Thomaston, Maine 04861
www.maineauthorspublishing.com

Printed in the United States of America

"Do any human beings ever realize life
while they live it—every, every minute?"

—THORNTON WILDER, *Our Town: A Play in Three Acts*

Table of Contents

Preface 3

Preface Notes 7

Chapter One: Folly Cove Sketches 9

Folly Cove Sketches Notes 16

Chapter Two: Jinnee's Rooms 19

Jinnee's Rooms Notes 26

Chapter Three: Jinnee's Books 31

Jinnee's Books Notes 40

Chapter Four: Thanksgiving 1962 45

Thanksgiving 1962 Notes 53

Chapter Five: Summer 1963 55

Summer 1963 Notes 60

Chapter Six: Life Drawing 63

Life Drawing Notes 70

Chapter Seven: Jinnee's Designs 73

Jinnee's Designs Notes 85

Chapter Eight: Neighbors 89

Neighbors Notes 96

Chapter Nine: Seascape 99

Seascape Notes 107

Chapter Ten: Late Summer 109

Late Summer Notes 114

Chapter Eleven: Early Spring 1964 117

Early Spring 1964 Notes 126

Chapter Twelve: Life Stories 129

Life Stories Notes 138

Acknowledgments 141

About the Author 143

Permissions 145

Folly Cove Sketches

Remembering Virginia Lee Burton

Jinnee and June Feeding Sheep at the Fence, 1967.
Photo credit David Vail.

Preface

IN LATE SUMMER 1961, MY PARENTS PACKED UP OUR STATION WAGON for a tour through New England. We planned to visit relatives, friends, and places they had left behind when they settled in Cleveland. I was seventeen and looking ahead to my first year at college that fall.

Our August stopover in Massachusetts introduced me to Uncle George and Aunt Jinnee—Virginia Lee Burton, the beloved award-winning author of *Mike Mulligan and His Steam Shovel* and *The Little House* and founder of the distinguished design cooperative Folly Cove Designers. Jinnee was my grandfather's younger sister, my great-aunt. Her husband, George Demetrios, was a sculptor and respected teacher.

Northeast of Boston, we reached Cape Ann, which extends like a lobster claw into the Atlantic. Near its northern tip is rock-bound Folly Point and next to it, Folly Cove, deep and narrow, rimmed with giant granite outcroppings. I immediately fell in love with Aunt Jinnee and Uncle George's unpretentious, artistic way of living: their small New England farmhouse, pale gray with yellow trim; Jinnee's big barn studio beside the house; the cozy kitchen. I admired the kitchen's hardwood floor and old-fashioned black stove, the living room's curtains and window-seat cushions with their hand-blocked prints, the garden's fresh lettuce, and the meadow's placid sheep—a bucolic contrast to suburban Ohio, but instantly it felt like home to me.

For the next seven years, Jinnee and George welcomed me for holidays, weekends, and summer stays. Those formative visits to Folly Cove, living among artists and learning by doing, helped me discover my own way. Now, as I read *Mike Mulligan* to my grandchildren, I recall with affection the inspiring woman behind her books. I appreciate the honesty, generosity, and grit she imparted by example as I developed from teenager to adult.

⁂

Jinnee published the Caldecott-winning *Little House* in 1942, during World War II, not long before I was born. That story and her other books deeply influenced my childhood and that of countless others. Anne Tyler, a Pulitzer Prize–winning novelist (*Breathing Lessons*, 1989) and literary critic, pinpointed the "one book that made you who you are today" in a *New York Times Book Review* feature:

"I do know how strange this sounds, but who I am today is all because of a picture book that was given me on my fourth birthday: Virginia Lee Burton's *The Little House*. I remember the first time my mother read it to me—how its message about the irreversible passage of time instantly hit home…. Nothing lasts forever, and…someday I would miss what I was now taking for granted."

For me, too, *The Little House* remains a story of time's inevitable passing, a chronicle of change, challenge, and renewal. *The Little House* honors the small farmhouse the Demetrios family relocated from busy Washington Street/Route 127 to a tranquil daisy-filled meadow. The book's pastel pages, curving lines, winding roads, and the arc of the rising and setting sun transport us through space and time, seasons and years, showing how change is both constant and cyclical. The natural world's patterns shape and alter *us*, as well as our surroundings. There's more than a little nostalgia here—a longing for the countryside, for family and simpler times—but also an acceptance that what we love must inevitably change and adapt or else disappear. Realistically, to keep what we love, we must pay attention and adjust while holding on to our memories.

I'm sharing these memories of Jinnee and George and my recollections of a vanishing time and place to honor them in our world of continual change. Certainly, nothing lasts forever.

⁂

During my Folly Cove stays, adjusting to unfamiliar surroundings and hoping to capture impressions, I truly took nothing for granted: I kept a journal and wrote several vignettes on the spot about people and experiences there. I was documenting a fascinating, appealing artist life. This memoir sketches my thoughts and feelings about Folly Cove then and now and considers Jinnee's artistic achievements and her life in her community setting. I've reflected on my own life experiences too and, with some background research, have begun to understand Jinnee's life and work more deeply. Chapter notes include relevant biographical details and provide references for further reading.

To illustrate my firsthand impressions of mid-century life at Folly Cove, I include letters, photos, drawings, and excerpts from interviews with Jinnee's family and fellow designers. Images from Jinnee's acclaimed books and Folly Cove Designers' creations link her personal history with earlier traditions in children's literature and printed textiles.

⁂

Folly Cove's unconventional way of life and its beautiful natural setting taught essential lessons, shaping my later approach to dancing, teaching, and writing: art should be woven into everyday experience. Every human being, with guidance, is capable of creating original work. Focus, discipline, and perseverance are necessary to achieve desired goals in any context. And finally, at its best, making art creates community and, in turn, community nourishes individual creativity. Both Jinnee and George modeled ways of crafting art and community that have inspired me for a lifetime.

In the summer of 1963, when I was nineteen, they presented me with a copy of iconic artist and master teacher Robert Henri's book *The Art Spirit*, which is still a touchstone for me. George had been acquainted with Robert Henri, a fellow student and kindred spirit of Charles Grafly, George's teacher and mentor at the Pennsylvania School of Fine Arts.

A memorable Henri quotation from *The Art Spirit* heads each of the following twelve chapters. Henri's teaching at the Art Students' League in New York recognized multiple and overlapping art communities, hailing "the great brotherhood of artists." However, he strongly encouraged individual experimentation, advising: "Blunder ahead with your own personal view."

Here's my personal view of Jinnee's and George's "art spirits"—complex and persistent, elegant and down-to-earth—and my account of how they influenced my life and the lives of countless others.

Preface Notes

Folly Cove, deep and narrow: Folly Cove was originally named Gallop's Folly, after a skipper who mistook the mouth of the cove for a larger harbor and, unable to turn around, wrecked his vessel on the rocks.

The one book that made you who you are today: *New York Times Book Review*, "By the Book," Anne Tyler, February 5, 2015.

***A copy of Robert Henri's book* The Art Spirit:** *The Art Spirit.* New York: Basic Books. 1923, 2007.

Blunder ahead with your own personal view: Henri, Robert, *The Art Spirit*, page 129.

Virginia Lee Demetrios (1909–1968), *Spring Lambs II*, 1951, ink on linen, linoleum block print. Collection of the Cape Ann Museum, Gloucester, MA.

CHAPTER ONE

Folly Cove Sketches

The sketch hunter…is learning to see and to understand—to enjoy.

O N A SUNNY JUNE AFTERNOON AFTER MY SOPHOMORE YEAR IN college, I arrived at Folly Cove to spend the summer. George and Jinnee were hosting a huge outdoor party near the apple tree and the little brook that ran behind the house and barn. They were roasting a lamb—or maybe multiple lambs—on spits, in the Greek style. An extended family of Burtons and "Demetrioi," with their Finnish neighbors and other friends, were enjoying a summer gathering. There were games for the little ones, plenty of soda, beer, and cocktails or wine for all, homemade stuffed grape leaf appetizers, music playing on the speakers at the barn window, and a warm, welcoming spirit. George was the gracious host, and most of the partygoers were adults—local artists, homemakers, teachers, and craftspeople.

I was nineteen, the only teenager. After a while, in the midst of this joyful and chaotic social gathering, I disappeared up to "my" bedroom overlooking the apple tree and roasting pit, and I cried.

I was excited to be there yet anxious about not belonging. Though I'd visited Jinnee and George before, during Thanksgiving and spring vacations, I felt dislocated and uncertain about how to fit into this unfamiliar mix. Lucia, Jinnee's older son Aris's then wife, came upstairs to find me. Our conversation was comforting. I appreciated her concern and the flattering way she restored my confidence. She told me that because I seemed poised, everyone assumed I felt secure and didn't realize I might be wary or feeling shy among my new "family."

A bit later, before the music and Greek line dancing began, I rejoined the festivities. These people seemed different from the

suburban adults I knew. I recognized the uniqueness of their personalities right away: they seemed emotionally open, eager to express
forthright opinions and unabashed enthusiasms. Clearly, they experienced social life in ways that I believed automatically vanished when
one became *adult*. They showed feelings! They *had* feelings! They
were dancing!

≈≈≈

I grew up in northeastern Ohio, the eldest of three sisters, during the
post–World War II '40s, '50s, and early '60s and enjoyed the privilege of a "normal" childhood, cared for and secure. The suburban
America of my childhood aspired to peace, security, and progress,
one consequence of that deeply disruptive war.

Looking back, I realize that I took for granted many advantages
and opportunities I considered commonplace. I attended outstand-
ing neighborhood schools from kindergarten through high school
in a beautiful, leafy setting. Our family appeared every Sunday
together at the First Unitarian Church. At home, we listened to a
wide range of recordings: Beethoven, Brubeck, Broadway musicals.
I wasn't pressed in any particular direction: I was free to follow my
early passions for horse figurines, Nancy Drew mysteries, and ballet
lessons. (I think my mother went by Dr. Benjamin Spock's tolerant
child-rearing theories.)

≈≈≈

In the early '60s, before urban renewal, the city of Gloucester,
Massachusetts, was a gritty North Shore fishing port. Rockport, its
neighboring village, was promoting an established reputation as a
picturesque seaside destination. The rural Folly Cove and Lanesville
neighborhoods lay between Gloucester and Rockport.

Cape Ann's scrubby, forested landscape, bordering the cold
Atlantic, is punctuated with isolated boulders called erratics, left
behind by receding glaciers, and abandoned granite quarries filled
with clear spring water. Historically, a few artists had shared this area
with farmers' and quarrymen's families, melding the sophistication

of urban outsiders with the charm of Yankee yeomen and the Nordic culture of Finnish immigrants who arrived in the late nineteenth and early twentieth centuries to work in the then-thriving granite industry. To me, its mid-twentieth-century inhabitants embodied features of this mixed heritage: on the one hand, they enthusiastically participated in communal endeavors such as summer barbecues, Saturday night potlucks, barn-raisings, and land-clearing bees, and on the other, they showed highly individualistic, independent spirits and a fondness for solitude.

⁂

How textured, how intense my experiences as a visitor there seemed, compared to my accustomed suburban or college dormitory existence! My sensory memories remain vivid. I eagerly breathed in the salt air and scents of a pebbly, seaweed-strewn shore. Dank lobster traps, soggy ropes green with algae, and the heavy, pungent odor of the fish wharf were new to me. Summer's hot, sunny, buzzing meadows and early September's gold-green light shimmering through the maples. The sounds of roaming sheep tearing at the high grass near the fenced-off garden. The maaa-ing and baaa-ing as lambs called to their mothers. The dawn bird chorus and seagulls' raucous calls. The barn swallows' dusky swoops.

Classical music at dinner. For holidays and parties, Finnish songs and Greek music after a meal in the barn: singing and dancing together. Later, back at college, I bought a vinyl recording of Greek music to energize my housekeeping chores—cleaning, bed changing, and laundry.

⁂

At Folly Cove, even everyday tasks became aesthetic: washing dishes, scrubbing clothes by hand, hanging them to dry, and finally, unbelievably to me today, ironing blouses! I harvested vegetables and learned to cook. Jinnee and George introduced me to Greek egg and lemon soup, yogurt, home-baked brown bread, and the completely foreign taste of braised fennel. French cheeses. And bottles of delicious wine.

We ate salads from the garden—tender green Boston lettuce, not iceberg, tossed with Italian olive oil, not bottled Wishbone dressing from the fridge! I baked dozens of Toll House cookies from scratch, following the recipe on the back of the yellow Nestlé's package.

⁂

Here is one of Jinnee's everyday recipes, as I copied it in my journal. It's still a supper favorite in our house. Garnish with a little fresh parsley, if you have it, and serve with buttered whole-wheat toast.

Folly Cove No-Fuss Greek Egg and Lemon Soup

1 can Campbell's chicken noodle soup (condensed)
3 eggs
Juice of 1 lemon

1. Prepare soup, adding a can of water. Heat in a pot on stove.
2. Beat three eggs (120 times) in a bowl.
3. Squeeze lemon and add the juice and a teeny bit of water to eggs. Stir.
4. Drop hot soup, spoonful by spoonful, into the mixture of eggs and lemon. Stir after each addition, until most of the broth is transferred to the bowl. When mixture is hot, pour it back into the pot on the stove, stirring all the time, and blend till slightly thickened and smooth over medium heat, just so it's boiling.
5. Turn off the heat when it bubbles, and serve immediately.
6. Never cover pot completely while standing.
7. For a larger amount, One (1) additional egg for each extra can of soup.

⁂

Shared meals and gatherings were occasions for interacting with new people, no matter that most of them were older or younger than I. I found this multi-generational dimension intriguing. I was paying attention to differences. I was realizing that people of all ages can be imperfect. I was discovering that some adults allow themselves to be openly annoyed, dejected, or elated. I was cultivating a sense of irony to save myself, on occasion, from dying of embarrassment. I was learning to define my boundaries and accept myself as I was and yet try for better.

Visiting Jinnee and George during my college years and living with them for some summer months energized and changed me. I attempted novel activities: drawing, lettering with India ink and pen, painting with watercolors, and throwing pottery on a neighbor's wheel. I learned how to eat a whole steamed lobster, including the delicacy of green tomalley. I mastered the art of taking a Finnish sauna with a diverse group of naked women. (And learned to pronounce sauna correctly: SOW-na.) I attended George's drawing class, absorbed design lessons from Jinnee, and learned to notice and to *see*. This generous community valued curiosity, attentiveness, and patience, and encouraged risk-taking.

⁓

Last year, for my birthday, my husband suggested framing several vintage Folly Cove Designer placemats. The mats, printed on cotton fabric, illustrate the design principles Jinnee taught: renderings of natural and everyday objects with variations in size, geometric arrangements, light and dark contrasts, and vivid colors—each one unique, detailed, and symmetrical.

A problem was that the placemats, along with my assortment of tablecloths and runners, had been well-used and showed it. I wasn't sure how they would look on a wall. Finally, I concluded that years of wear only enhanced their authenticity and appeal. I washed and ironed five different designs and delivered them to a framer.

Matted in white and framed with light birch, they are daily reminders of the skilled craftspeople who created them and the community I remember so vividly. I admire the lively motifs of Jinnee's blue-on-white "Spring Lambs II" (1951) and her green-on-white "George's Garden" (1964), Louise Kenyon's yellow "New

Virginia Lee Demetrios (1909–1968), *Reducing*, 1949,
ink on linen, linoleum block print. Collection of
the Cape Ann Museum, Gloucester, MA.

England Flowers" (1943), and Eino Natti's ocean-hued "Yo Heave Ho" lobsterman (1953). My favorite, perhaps, is Jinnee's playfully self-referential "Reducing" (1949) in red on white: a well-padded fitness buff pursues her slenderizing goal through a series of vigorous calisthenics, from toe-touching to jump-roping.

***

Designer and neighbor Eino Natti once assured me that a visitor to Cape Ann will always return. Maybe he was referring to the area's irresistible natural beauty or the draw of its people. Or possibly to a mysterious, invisible magnetism: according to New Age theorists, Cape Ann is located on a "ley line" or pathway of spiritual forces, positive and negative, that affects everyone along it.

In any case, I've certainly returned to Folly Cove numerous times over the years, in all seasons—in person, and even more often, in memory.

***

Folly Cove Sketches Notes

The sketch hunter...is learning to see and to understand— to enjoy: Henri, *The Art Spirit*, page 17.

Sketch: n, (3a) a short literary composition somewhat resembling the short story and the essay but intentionally slight in treatment, discursive in style, and familiar in tone. *Merriam-Webster.com Dictionary*, https://www.merriam-webster.com/dictionary/sketch.

Nordic culture of the Finnish immigrants: Quarry workers and stone cutters from Finland and Sweden arrived in Lanesville and Folly Cove as the industry thrived from the 1870s through 1930.

I admire the lively motifs: For more information and photos, see Folly Cove Designers, Cape Ann Historical Association exhibit catalog, May 7 through October 31, 1996, reprinted 2017. An overview of Designers' history, members' biographies, and gallery of their works.

Virginia Lee Demetrios (1909–1968), *Swing Tree*, undated, ink on linen, linoleum block print. Collection of the Cape Ann Museum, Gloucester, MA.

CHAPTER TWO

Jinnee's Rooms

*The thing is for each individual…to discover [her]self
as a human being, with needs of [her] own.*

JINNEE'S BIG OLD BARN STUDIO, SHINGLED GRAY WITH YELLOW TRIM TO match the house, stood only a few yards away, across a flagstone terrace. The interior of the barn was Jinnee's domain, overflowing with the tools, accumulated over decades, and the products of her art—wood carvings, textiles, and original drawings for her award-winning books.

A large skylight at the north end illuminated a drawing board, typewriter table, and swivel chair. Various seashells, dried flowers, a jay's wing, and a crab shell collected on her frequent walks in woods and along the shore, and several ashtrays, lay scattered on Jinnee's table and nearby windowsill. Drawings were tacked up here and there on the bare, rough wood walls alongside newspaper clippings, correspondence with editors, and a framed letter from her half-brother Harold, my grandfather.

Their father, Alfred Burton, beloved by them both, had been a civil engineer and cartographer, a precise draftsman and gifted amateur watercolor artist, and professor and dean at the Massachusetts Institute of Technology. George's handsome bronze bust of Alfred Burton surveyed Jinnee's studio from the mantel of the imposing fieldstone fireplace.

A long shelf nearby displayed Jinnee's books, beginning with *ChooChoo*, which appeared in 1937, followed by *Mike Mulligan and His Steam Shovel*, *The Little House*, *Katy and the Big Snow*, *Calico the Wonder Horse*, *Song of Robin Hood*, *The Emperor's New Clothes*, and *Maybelle the Cable Car*. The most recent, *Life Story*, published in the spring of 1962, completed the collection. Many of her books had also been translated into Japanese, French, and Danish.

Dusty conglomerations of paint cans, bottles filled with brushes and pencils and ink pens, piles of small sketchbooks, and a couple of sample covers drafted for the *New Yorker* crowded the narrow shelves toe-nailed between studs. In one corner stood a large, beautiful, multi-paneled wooden screen that Jinnee had adorned with images of the brook and woods behind the barn in four seasons. An ironing board leaned against the wall.

A recently acquired television set, its screen modestly veiled by a small Persian rug, sat on its own table. George had lately consented to the television, to which he promptly became addicted.

At the barn's far end, next to her flatbed proof press and a hand-operated Acorn press for printing on cotton fabric, Jinnee had gathered block-printing tools, ink, and uncut linoleum blocks. Her Folly Cove Designer linoleum blocks hung from hooks on the wall, stowed away or ready for printing.

Several yellowed, dog-eared three-by-five note cards were thumb-tacked to the exposed studs above a second drawing board, including a type-written quotation attributed to George Eliot:

"The Essence of Friendship: Ah, the comfort, the inexhaustible comfort, of feeling safe with a person: having neither to weigh thoughts nor measure words, but to pour them out, just as they are, chaff and grain, knowing that a faithful hand will take and sift them, keep what is worth keeping, and then, with the breath of kindness, blow the rest away."

I shared this yearning to be accepted, and I copied down that thought for myself.

⋘⋙

Along the main portion of the barn stretched roomier shelves containing an extensive collection of 78 rpm classical record albums, various books, woven baskets, and papers. Jinnee had designed and carved an intricate mahogany case for the nearby phonograph. On the end wall, steep, narrow stairs led to a hayloft with a small window overlooking the backyard. There, a speaker was set under the eaves. On soft summer evenings, as barn swallows swooped to catch mosquitoes in mid-air, we would sit on the stone patio at the huge table of polished, locally quarried granite, dining to Mozart or Bach and enjoying George's selection of the best French wines.

≪≪≋⌐

Decades later, I discovered Jinnee's correspondence with my grand-father Harold in files stored in my parents' attic. I located some of Jinnee's letters to her English mother, Jeanne D'Orge, née Lena Yates, when I visited the Cherry Foundation in Carmel, California. Further information about Jeanne D'Orge's extraordinary life and work, her poetry, plays, and painting, helped me appreciate in a new way the importance of the barn studio in her daughter's life.

Jeanne D'Orge's story is complicated. She abandoned her birth name, Lena Yates, and later her married name, Lena Burton, as well as the *nom-de-plume* Lena Dalkeith that she had attached to writings she'd published in the early 1900s: three books of stories and plays for children. She and Alfred Burton married in England, a decade after his first wife, Harold's mother, died. Then the couple, accom-panied by Jeanne's mother, arrived in the United States. However, after fifteen years of marriage, Jeanne left their Massachusetts home with the couple's three children and traveled cross-country to settle in California. Alfred Burton soon retired from MIT to follow them.

But when Jinnee was a junior in high school in Carmel-by-the-Sea, Jeanne scandalously deserted the family to live with her lover, Carl Cherry, one of Burton's former students at MIT and twenty years her junior. In the aftermath, Alfred Burton returned to Boston, and the children became estranged from their mother. Although, like her older sister and younger brother, Jinnee was deeply affected by the abandonment, as an adult she was able to reconcile with her mother.

Sometime in the 1940s, Jinnee renewed contact with Jeanne. By then, Jinnee was a thirty-something wife and mother herself and a successful author/illustrator. Perhaps then she could better under-stand her mother's impulse for choosing creative passions over family commitments. She welcomed Jeanne's attention and advice.

Jinnee's own desire for freedom to experiment artistically became evident in a letter to her mother in which she outlined a scheme to enlarge the small house at Folly Cove. In the margin, Jinnee sketched a design:

> Every once in a while we talk about the addition to the house…my room and kitchen…. Got an idea the other day…. Why not just add a smaller edition of this house to one end? It's better than what the architect had planned, before *we* or rather *you*, said I should have a room of my own…

The apparent reference was to Virginia Woolf's classic 1929 essay, *A Room of One's Own*, recognizing the need for a woman to stake out personal territory for writing or any kind of art-making. The more open domain Jinnee envisioned, a bedroom above and an enlarged kitchen below, was the house I came to love. For me, too, a workspace of my own within my home eventually became necessary.

⸻

In 1956, a decade after writing that letter to her mother, and as the Folly Cove Designers' printed textiles were gaining nationwide commercial success, Jinnee was corresponding with her brother Harold. She enthusiastically described her next plans for expansion. This time, she envisioned enlarging her seasonal barn studio as a year-round multi-purpose workspace. Previously, she had used the uninsulated barn only in warmer weather. In colder seasons, she was limited to the house, writing and sketching at a table in the small living room. She proposed dividing the barn's new addition to accommodate her wide-ranging artistic pursuits.

> …now it shall be called the "barn-studio." The old barn part will be used for Folly Cove Designing and writing books…. The new studio part will be for painting and wood carving which I have not been able to do for twenty years…so besides

opening and enlarging my "barn" I am opening and enlarging my point of view and way of working…

And, writing to her mother in the same week, Jinnee's eager anticipation of the new workroom's possibilities was unmistakable:

The BARN-STUDIO is almost done and it is beautiful. Eino and I worked like mad cleaning and polishing and getting it ready for the Folly Cove Designers meeting last Thursday. The old part has never been so neated up.… I don't want to disturb it. I just sit around and admire all the beautiful clean spaces…

The new part I will keep pure…just do the things I want to…and not for money. The old part is for block printing, designing, and writing books.… I think I will probably have to work in the old part to pay for the new part…but that's alright.

Like Robert Henri, Jinnee was more "interested in art as a way of living, not a way of making a living." Nonetheless, the need to make a living persisted, and she was flourishing as the family's primary breadwinner.

Not long after the barn-studio renovations were complete, Jinnee described to Harold her next book-in-progress, provisionally titled *Life Story*, which turned out to be her final creation.

For the last six months I have been having a wonderful time doing "research" for a new book which involves the study of geology, biology, zoology, botany, paleontology—in fact almost all of the "ologies"—plus a week in the American Museum of Natural History in New York, drawing dinosaurs. Naturally this would be a children's book and mostly pictures with a very simple text.… And anyway whether I do this book or not I am having fun and learning a great deal.

Jinnee spent years researching, writing, and revising *Life Story*. Finally, on May 9, 1962, she declared to Harold:

> At last the book is done. Publication was…May 6, which was a Sunday, so my publishers [Houghton Mifflin] gave me a party in the Skyline Room of the Boston Museum of Science…. Everything went smoothly and I'm glad it is all over. I'm sending you and Selma a copy.

Harold praised the book at length and closed his letter with affectionate approval: "I am proud of the result and proud of you…!"

She replied, "Thank you for your good letter and for the time and thought you put into writing it. I have framed it and keep it in my barn studio where I can look at it whenever I need encouragement."

This was the congratulatory letter from my grandfather framed on the wall by her drawing board under the skylight. The half-siblings had each lost mothers at a young age. Their father connected them with bonds of mutual affection and respect. Both siblings had achieved prominence in their fields, Jinnee in the arts and Harold in jurisprudence.

My grandfather's warm note typified his patient, considerate interest in his family and in his grandchildren's projects, too. Each June, he and my grandmother arrived in Cleveland from Washington, D.C., in their Buick roadster, its windshield covered with splattered bugs, to attend my middle sister's and my annual ballet recitals. They returned each Thanksgiving and Christmas for family holiday dinners. Throughout childhood, we grandchildren regularly received small packets of colorful postage stamps he thought we'd like, and he encouraged us with handwritten notes illustrated with whimsical stick-figure drawings.

<hr/>

After the success of *Life Story*, Jinnee decided to erect one more "room of her own": a small cottage, a pre-fab architectural folly, on her plot of land at the tip of Folly Point, near the family's favorite swimming, sunbathing, fishing, and picnicking spot. Perched on the rocks above the sea, the tiny cottage represented both a treat—that is, a reward for her long labors—and a retreat, a hideaway. For Jinnee, this freedom was a fitting compensation: she could leave the house and drive to the cottage at the Point in her new gray Mustang convertible without having to justify what she'd do there: write, sketch, contemplate her world, or sleep.

The simple modular cabin sat on cement blocks on top of ledge rock. Its rafters were reinforced with steel ties from roof to wall as protection against northerly storms off the ocean. Jinnee equipped the place with Spartan essentials: a built-in couch/daybed for naps, a plywood drawing surface, a small woodstove, a kerosene lamp. Windows on three walls gave a panoramic view of sea and sky from the built-in desk. On bright mornings, the sun rose from under the horizon to hang over the vast expanse of the Atlantic Ocean.

However active Jinnee's life seemed, and however magnetically she drew family, friends, and neighbors around her, she guarded her work hours closely and insisted on time alone. From early in her marriage, she and George, who required his own workspace, relied on house-keeping support from local women who also cared for their young sons, Aris and Mike. Aili Runsala was the most recent in a succession of Finnish neighbors who helped with cooking, cleaning, and other chores.

The house addition, barn studio, writing cottage, and Jinnee's solitary walks in Cape Ann's woodsy natural environment enlarged her private sphere, providing treasured freedom and time for exploring fresh "points of view and ways of working."

Jinnee's Rooms Notes

The thing is for each individual...to discover [her] self as a human being, with needs of [her] own: Henri, *The Art Spirit*, page 211.

Their father, Alfred Burton, was a civil engineer: Harold and his older brother, Arnold, were the children of Alfred Edgar Burton's first family. In 1884, Alfred Burton married the remarkable Gertrude Hitz and fathered two sons, Arnold (1885) and Harold (1888). Gertrude died of tuberculosis in a Swiss sanitarium in 1896 at the age of thirty-four, and the boys, aged ten and seven, were sent to board at the progressive Allen School in Newton, Massachusetts.

Alfred Burton was a member of the faculty of the Massachusetts Institute of Technology beginning in 1884 and later served as dean until 1922. He died in 1935.

Alfred Burton married the extraordinary Lena Yates in 1906. Jinnee was the second of three children of Burton's second marriage to Lena: Christine, Virginia Lee, and Ross Alexander. Jinnee was born in 1909, the year my grandfather Harold graduated from college, so she was closer in age to Harold's daughter, my mother, than to her half-brother.

For a biography of Jinnee's mother, Jeanne D'Orge (Lena Yates Burton), and a comprehensive look at her poetry and painting, see Wilgress, Jane, *Better than Beauty: The Life and Work of Jeanne D'Orge*, Park Place Publications, Pacific Grove, CA, 2004.

For the complete story of Alfred Burton's first family, see Vail, June, *The Passion of Perfection: Gertrude Hitz Burton's Modern Victorian Life*, Maine Authors Publishing, Thomaston, Maine, 2017.

A type-written quotation attributed to George Eliot: The Essence of Friendship was actually written by Dinah Maria Mulock Craik (1826–1887). The excerpt appears in her 1859 novel, *A Life for a Life*, Chapter 16.

To live with her lover, Carl Cherry: Feeling stifled and unhappy in her marriage, Jeanne D'Orge left Boston for California in 1920, taking her children with her. A year later, Burton retired from MIT and followed the family to Carmel.

In Carmel-by-the-Sea, Jeanne fell in love with Carl Cherry, an eccentric inventor twenty years her junior and more than thirty years younger than Burton, who had been his professor at MIT. When Jeanne left the house late one night to live with Cherry, the family was irreparably fragmented. The children, aged sixteen, fourteen, and ten, found temporary homes with family and friends. Burton returned to Boston from California in 1925.

Jeanne, already an author and poet, had published in Alfred Kreymborg's literary magazine *Others: A Magazine of the New Verse*, as well as in *Scribner's* and *Poetry* magazines. She had read her work at the *Others* poetry reading in the famous 1913 Armory Show, along with William Carlos Williams, Marianne Moore, and Wallace Stevens.

Jeanne began to paint while Cherry occupied himself with his inventions, one of which became the Cherry Blind Rivet. Cherry's invention revolutionized the aircraft and shipbuilding industries and was in great demand during World War II. While income from the Cherry Blind Rivet patent later provided the couple with enough money to live lavishly, it changed their lifestyle little. They bought more books and more phonograph records and established a foundation. Cherry died of spinal cancer in 1947.

Now it shall be called the "barn-studio": letter from VLB to HHB, November 10, 1956.

The BARN-STUDIO is almost done: letter from VLB to Jeanne D'Orge, November 3, 1956.

For the last six months: letter from VLB to HHB, November 10, 1956.

At last the book is done: letter from VLB to HHB, May 9, 1962.

I am proud of the result: letter from HHB to VLB, May 18, 1962.

Thank you for your good letter: letter from VLB to HHB, May 29, 1962.

Both siblings had achieved prominence in their fields: Harold Hitz Burton's career in politics began in Cleveland, Ohio, where, as a Republican, he was elected to the Ohio state legislature in 1928. He served the city of Cleveland as law director, 1930–31; acting mayor, 1931–32; and mayor, 1935–40. In 1940 he was elected to the U.S. Senate. In 1945, President Harry Truman, with whom he had worked across the aisle in the Senate, appointed him to the United States Supreme Court.

Their young sons, Aris and Mike: Aristides Burton Demetrios (1932–2021) is a renowned contemporary sculptor of bronze fountains and sculptures, large scale outdoor stainless steel sculptures, and painted steel sculptures commissioned for public pavilions—for example, in California, on the Stanford University campus and at the Monterey Bay Aquarium. His work is also exhibited in museums, galleries, and residential gardens throughout the United States.

Michael Burton Demetrios (1935-2016) was a graduate of Harvard Business School, and an entrepreneurial leader as president of Marine World Africa USA for more than twenty years. He had theatrical flair, an infectious laugh, and a generous heart.

As adults both Aris and Mike settled in California.

Virginia Lee Demetrios (1909–1968), *Little House*,
undated, ink on linen, linoleum block print.
Collection of the Cape Ann Museum, Gloucester, MA.

CHAPTER THREE

Jinnee's Books

It is a question of saying the thing that a person has to say.

J INNEE HAD RESERVED THE OLD PART OF THE BARN FOR DESIGNING block prints and writing books, projects whose income supported the family. As I leafed through her books, lined up on the shelf beside the fireplace, they seemed to chronicle twenty-five years of creative effort, each one a fresh take on storytelling through images and text.

Before I met Jinnee, my parents had read me her stories, and I learned many by heart. Today, nine of them line my own bookshelf at home, some in multiple copies—hardcovers now falling apart, inscribed copies presented to my grandparents or to me, and more recent paperback editions personalized with my young sons' scribbles.

Before I could read the words, I grasped the images with a child's curiosity about what would happen next. Shapes and colors flowed with thrilling speed on each page or across broad two-page spreads. I understood later that Jinnee drew the images first, tacking them to the wall as a visual storyboard, before shaping the accompanying text.

The stories introduced attention-grabbing plots and characters—human, animal, and machine. We meet a boy who comes up with a solution to a problem no adults can solve, and another who comes out with a truth no adults will speak; there are plucky, friendly machines and their human coworkers; a super-smart horse who foils evil rustlers; lumbering dinosaurs; and a charming Robin Hood.

As a child, I hadn't noticed that Jinnee's books showcased female heroes who could inspire girls like me to star in our own "her-stories." As I read them now, I realize that Jinnee's female protagonists—Little House, clever Calico, ChooChoo the engine, Maybelle, Katy, and, most famously, Mary Anne, Mike Mulligan's steam shovel—anthropomorphize a house, a horse, and various pieces of heavy equipment as smart, determined, and tenacious as Jinnee herself. They're hard workers who take pride in their accomplishments. And they don't take everyday things for granted. They recognize both the beneficial and unfortunate changes time brings, and when put to the test, they're able to adapt: if they become obsolete, they reinvent themselves—a steam shovel can become a furnace to warm the town hall. They cope. They endure.

Today, I interpret Jinnee's books as "saying the things that [she] had to say," as Robert Henri put it. The stories convey messages about comforting familiarity and peaceful stability in our lives: the grandness of nature's beauty, the satisfaction of hard work, the importance of a home, and the need for flexibility in the face of inevitable change. These themes appear again and again. Often, they intersect and combine, explicitly or subtly, personified in strong female protagonists.

⁓

Each of Jinnee's five earliest published stories, from *ChooChoo* through *Katy and the Big Snow*, highlights these themes. From her late twenties to her mid-thirties, Jinnee wrote and illustrated these five books in six years: *ChooChoo*, 1937; *Mike Mulligan and His Steam Shovel*, 1939; *Calico the Wonder Horse, or the Saga of Stewy Stinker*, 1941; *The Little House*, 1942; and *Katy and the Big Snow*, 1943. Such astonishing creative energy during the early years of her marriage, raising young children!

The books bolstered household finances while giving Jinnee a chance to innovate ways of visual storytelling. For example, *ChooChoo* and *Calico the Wonder Horse, or the Saga of Stewy Stinker* offer strikingly different, imaginative methods for illustrating themes of home and community.

ChooChoo's images, rendered in black and white in broad, sweeping conté crayon strokes, suggest the train's breakneck speed as the curious, strong-willed little engine jumps the tracks by herself but realizes after her wild ride that "running away isn't much fun." She changes her mind and returns home to her friends in the train yard. *ChooChoo* was often my childhood bedtime story: I loved Jim, the engineer, Archibald, the conductor, and especially ChooChoo's fireman, Oley. For some reason, my younger sister called her comfort blanket "Oley."

Four years after *ChooChoo*, Jinnee was again exploring black-and-white graphics, this time not with crayon but on scratchboard panels, a time-consuming technique that involves coating a white surface with black ink, then scratching it away to draw each image. *Calico the Wonder Horse* comes to life printed on tinted papers—yellow, tan, dark green, orange, pink, dark pink, green, and back to yellow. Mimicking the look of the Sunday comics, the colors convey the story's changing moods.

Cowboy Hank and his horse Calico ("She wasn't very pretty… but she was very smart. She was the smartest, fastest horse in all of Cactus County.") track the villainous cattle rustler Stewy Stinker, who sports a droopy handlebar mustache. With his wacky, thieving gang of Bad Men, Stinker hatches a plot to hijack a stagecoach filled with Christmas presents for the Cactus County children. After an exciting chase, Hank and Calico outwit the gang and save the presents, and all ends well when Stinker recants from his jail cell on Christmas Eve, crying, "I didn't know I was that mean.… I'm never going to be bad anymore." The bad guys join the community Christmas party in the schoolhouse: the rustlers promise to be good, Hank is elected sheriff, and Calico becomes his deputy sheriff. "Once again everybody was happy and contented in Cactus County," home again, safe and sound. I cherish the copy Jinnee gave me, "With love and best wishes," before I left Folly Cove to fly home to Ohio in September 1963.

Mike Mulligan still seems to be Jinnee's most well-known book, after eighty years in print, beloved by generations of parents, kids, and librarians. Mary Anne and Mike crash through the book's red dustcover, and inside, Popperville's S-curving roads, MaryAnne's spiraling excavations, and even Mike's rocking chair suggest constant movement. The horizontal format keeps most of the color images small in relation to the surrounding white space and the accompanying text. A few larger high-energy illustrations fill whole pages. The end papers' detailed drawings of Mike's steam shovel beckon young readers or listeners to look more closely.

Illustration from *Mike Mulligan and his Steam Shovel* by Virginia Lee Burton. Copyright 1939 by Virginia Lee Burton, renewed 1967 by Virginia Lee Demetrios. Reprinted by permission of Clarion Books, an imprint of HarperCollins Publishers LLC.

The plot revolves around a little boy who solves the problem that stumps the grownups: how to extract Mary Anne, Mike's technologically old-fashioned but still sturdy steam shovel, from the cellar hole she has so skillfully dug for the new town hall. "Why couldn't we leave Mary Anne in the cellar and build the new town hall over her? Let her be the furnace," the child suggests.

Mike Mulligan sends positive messages: first, every problem may present a challenge, but every challenge can become an opportunity! And second, everyone in Popperville has something to contribute— young children, old townspeople, and even older steam shovels.

Once again
she was lived in
and taken care of.
39

Illustration from *The Little House* by Virginia Lee Burton,
renewed 1969 by Aristides Burton Demetrios and Michael
Burton Demetrios. Reprinted by permission of Clarion
Books, an imprint of HarperCollins Publishers LLC.

If you look carefully at the cover illustration of *The Little House*, you
see on the front walk, just under the doorstep, the book's subtitle:
Her-Story. The sturdy rose-colored Little House, naively curious
about city life, imagines exciting, cosmopolitan adventures. When
urban development expands unchecked all around her, she becomes
disillusioned: rushing traffic and tall buildings obscure sunlight and
stars. She's overjoyed when she's finally rescued and returned to the
country to "settle down on her new foundation." No longer tempted
by the promise of urban progress, and delighted to be lived in and
cared for once more, she follows the arc of the sun each new day and
eases into the seasonal rhythms of spring, summer, fall, and winter.

The Little House taught lessons about time and change and has been cited by advocates of environmentalism, social revitalization, and historic preservation. The story hints at a longing for simpler times, living close to nature, but it also suggests that while valuing the past in a fast-changing world, we must be prepared to take action and adapt. Jinnee dedicated this story to "Dorgie," her sons' nickname for their dad, George Demetrios. The family's own little house was moved and modified over the years according to changing needs.

The 1943 Caldecott committee awarded *The Little House* its annual medal for "distinguished illustrations in a picture book and… excellence of pictorial presentation for children."

<hr/>

Katy and the Big Snow appeared in the year I was born and, along with the others, was familiar childhood reading in snowy northeast Ohio. Katy the snowplow is a "beautiful red crawler tractor" outfitted with a V-shaped snowplow for the heaviest winter work. "She was very big and very strong and she could do a lot of things"—a mechanical equivalent to the wartime heroine Rosie the Riveter.

After a huge blizzard, Katy succeeds in clearing snow from the entire city of Geopolis. Colorful maps, compasses, and diagrams of heavy machinery help us trace her snowy path as she moves north, south, east, and west. Downtown we find city hall, the police department, library, high school, church, and post office. We follow bright red Katy's progress in opening a path through a vast white expanse, methodically nosing from the top corner of the left-hand page to the lower corner of the right, making headway through the deep, wide snowdrifts that cover two pages. A community-spirited worker, Katy turns toward home only after she has cleared all the roads and streets.

<hr/>

I searched for a copy of *Robin Hood* for years before finding a disclaimed library copy. Jinnee's exquisite illustrations for a collection of traditional English ballads, *Song of Robin Hood* was published after the war's end, in 1947. It is neither an original story nor a conventional children's book, but an artistic *tour de force* illuminating Anne Malcolmson's selected Robin Hood ballads and Grace Castagnetta's piano arrangements. It was a labor of love honoring the traditional music and culture of her mother's native England. Jinnee commented that *Robin Hood* "took me three years to complete and gave me a chance to develop and practice my theories on design."

Robin Hood's filigreed graphics refine the black-and-white scratchboard technique Jinnee first used with Stewy Stinker. Here, her detailed images resemble medieval manuscripts. Jinnee played with stylized and abstract renderings of natural subjects—forests, flowers, birds, and animals, and people, depicting the evil Sheriff of Nottingham and beloved Sherwood Forest dwellers Robin, Maid Marian, Little John, and Allen-a-Dale. For her *Robin Hood* illustrations, Jinnee received the 1948 Caldecott Honor prize.

✿

If Jinnee paid tribute to her mother, Jeanne D'Orge, in *Robin Hood*, two years later she acknowledged her father, Alfred Burton, in *The Emperor's New Clothes* (1949). Jinnee called it "one of my favorite Hans Christian Andersen stories my father read aloud to us." She drew her own version with rococo pastel curlicues and a light, humorous touch. As in *Mike Mulligan*, a child saves the day, this time by speaking truth to power: he reveals the vain emperor and his sycophantic court as imposters by calling out the ludicrously obvious: "The Emperor has no clothes!"

✿

In the '50s, Jinnee made several visits to California to help her aging mother relocate to a comfortable living situation. Her book *Maybelle the Cable Car* (1952) is set in San Francisco, recalling Jinnee's home as a young art student. Like some of Jinnee's other stories, *Maybelle* supports reimagining instead of discarding what has served in the past. The story champions the mechanical ingenuity, sedate pace, and charm of the city's fabled cars. Maybelle maneuvers the city's steep hills far better than Big Bill, one of the modern buses. In fact, the San Francisco Citizens' Committee to Save the Cable Cars recruited the popular *Maybelle* for its successful grassroots campaign to enshrine the cable cars as San Francisco icons.

Ten years elapsed before Jinnee's last book, *Life Story*, appeared in 1962, shortly after I first met her. *Life Story* chronicles change on a cosmic scale, recounting the sweeping epic of life on earth from its beginnings up to now—literally, until today, this very moment. To me, it seems like a culmination of Jinnee's art and ideas, beginning "Eons and eons ago our Sun was born, one of the millions and billions of stars that make up our galaxy, called the Milky Way," and ending this morning: "at dawn.... The time is now and the place wherever you are."

Life Story is complex and layered, yet clearly explained for young readers: "Our Earth was born millions and billions of years ago, one of the Sun's family of nine planets. Our Earth is the third planet out from the Sun. It is not the biggest planet, nor is it the smallest, but to us it is the most important, for this is where we live."

As a third-grader, I could reel off my own planetary address, starting with home and expanding as far as I could imagine: Daleford Road, Shaker Heights, Cleveland, Ohio, the United States of America, the Northern Hemisphere, the planet Earth, the solar system, the Milky Way, the universe. *Life Story* reverses this perspective in time and space. Starting from a galactic point of view, the text and illustrations progressively narrow our focus, until gradually, spiraling through eras from the Paleozoic through the Mesozoic, Cenozoic, and Paleolithic, it zeroes in on everyday lives in homes and communities.

In a May 1968 interview, just five months before her death, Jinnee explained in her quick, assertive way the ideas behind this challenging project and her process of fusing science, art, and text. Although she originally set out to create a book on nature, the task grew all-encompassing as research led her deeper into her subject.

Life Story connects us, here and now, with everything everywhere that has gone before, appreciating each human being's unique, impermanent place in evolution's immense "ever new, ever changing, ever wondrous" pattern. It presents an existential challenge: starting today, each one of us has a chance to create our own life stories in our own small realms. In that process, we help shape the whole earth's future, too, because the fate of our planet, now so altered by human interference with natural changes, depends on our individual choices and collective actions.

Like nearly all of Jinnee's books, *Life Story* shows readers the way home. I believe that at a deep level, Jinnee's stories spring from her personal experience and observations and reveal her values as a strong, problem-solving, compassionate truth-teller with a reverence for tradition. Each stylistically distinct book confirms Jinnee's joy in making art and living life in the home and community she helped create.

Illustration from *Life Story* by Virginia Lee Burton. Copyright 1962
by Virginia Lee Demetrios, renewed 1990 by Aristides Burton
Demetrios and Michael Burton Demetrios. Reprinted by permission
of Clarion Books, an imprint of HarperCollins Publishers LLC.

Jinnee's Books Notes

It is a question of saying the thing that a person has to say:
Henri, *The Art Spirit*, page 137.

All titles published by Houghton Mifflin Harcourt Co.
    ChooChoo: The Story of a Little Engine Who Ran Away, 1937
    Mike Mulligan and His Steam Shovel, 1939
    Calico the Wonder Horse, or the Saga of Stewy Stinker, 1941
    The Little House, 1942
    Katy and the Big Snow, 1943
    Song of Robin Hood, 1947
    The Emperor's New Clothes, 1949
    Maybelle the Cable Car, 1952
    *Life Story/ The Story of Life on Our Earth from its Beginning
        Up to Now*, 1962

Jinnee drew **ChooChoo** with dynamic gestures in broad strokes, similar to her action-filled sketches accompanying the drama and dance reviews by the Boston *Evening Transcript*'s legendary critic Henry Taylor Parker (known as "H.T.P."). Vertical and large scale, the book's double-page spreads heighten and magnify the story's sense of action. The text is shaped and integrated into the images.

In 1928, after a year of study at the San Francisco School of Fine Arts, Jinnee moved from California to Boston to care for her father, who had broken his leg. She "kept house" for him in their shared studio apartment in an artists' cooperative on Beacon Hill's Joy Street while she was employed as a sketcher by Boston's daily afternoon newspaper, the *Evening Transcript*. At nineteen, she had found success illustrating the *Transcript's* drama reviews and weekend edition feature stories. In the fall of 1930, she enrolled in the Boston Museum School's

Saturday morning drawing class, taught by handsome, magnetic thirty-four-year-old George Demetrios. She had just turned twenty-one. The two exceptional artists were married the following spring, and a year later, with their infant son Aristides, they made Cape Ann and Folly Cove their home.

Jinnee called **Calico**, originally subtitled the *Saga of Stewy Slinker*, her "attempt to wean Aris and Mike away from comic books." The later "uncensored" editions of *Calico* used the villain's intended name, Stewy Stinker.

Mike Mulligan is the only children's book I know with a footnote. At the bottom of this key page, we see *Acknowledgements to Dickie Birkenbush* (sic). I learned later that Dickie, thirteen, came up with the transformative solution just as Jinnee was wrestling with possible endings. She was visiting his mother, Jean (Albertson) Berkenbush, at Chestnut Hill Farm in West Newbury, Massachusetts. "The Farm," as it was known earlier in the twentieth century, was a voluntary community founded by Dickie's grandparents, Hazel and Ralph Albertson. Aris Demetrios commented in an interview on his mother's progressive, socially responsible spirit: "There was…a movement… in Boston in the '20s and '30s and my mother was certainly in that…. She was going out to Albertson's farm…. She was a fierce believer in social justice."

The Little House mirrors Americana themes in the arts and literature prevalent throughout the '30s and early '40s: Grant Wood's 1930 *American Gothic*; the premiere of Thornton Wilder's *Our Town* in 1938; Martha Graham's 1940 tribute to Emily Dickinson, *Letter to the World*; and Aaron Copeland's 1944 *Appalachian Spring* come immediately to mind.

Robin Hood took me three years to complete: VLB autobiography, small booklet, 1962, Houghton Mifflin.

Songs of Robin Hood's illustrations convey Jinnee's lifelong affection for English music. She recalled that her English mother's traditions influenced her early childhood years in Newton Center, Massachusetts, until she was about ten. Jeanne D'Orge organized events there with "English folk songs and folk dancing around a Maypole, and celebrat[ed] Twelfth Night when everyone dressed in costumes and the neighbors came in to sing and dance and 'wassail' the old apple trees."

Maybelle the Cable Car appeared as Jinnee and the Folly Cove Designers were expanding their textile production and marketing, basking in the national prominence of Lord and Taylor advertisements and a *Life* magazine feature.

Life Story conceives the development of life on earth as a play in five acts with a "Cast of Leading Animals and Plants" backed up by a chorus of additional "Supporting Players." The production begins with a prologue and concludes with an epilogue. A team of narrators is spotlighted stage right in front of the red curtain. An astronomer and a geologist guide the prologue. Paleontologists announce the first three acts. A historian explains the fourth. And Virginia Lee Burton, grandmother and author, describes the final colorful scenes. She explains that "the last act in my latest book, *Life Story*, tells the story of our life here in Folly Cove."

Lee Natti, Jinnee's early editor, friend, and Designer colleague, wrote that "the demanding process of research and writing was exhausting to [Jinnee], physically and creatively. ...As she could not do another book, it is appropriate that *Life Story* was her final, all-encompassing creation." Natti, Lee, "Virginia Lee Burton's Dynamic Sense of Design" in, Natti, Lee Kingman, ed., *The Illustrator's Notebook*, The Horn Book, Inc., 1978.

In a May 1968 interview: interview with Boston College Professor Albert Duhamel aired by WGBH, Boston Public Television.

Virginia Lee Demetrios (1909–1968), *George's Garden*, 1964, ink on linen, linoleum block print. Collection of the Cape Ann Museum, Gloucester, MA.

CHAPTER FOUR

Thanksgiving 1962

An interest in the subject, something you want to say definitely about the subject, this is the first condition of a portrait.

JINNEE AND GEORGE HAD INVITED ME TO VISIT DURING THE Thanksgiving break in my freshman year at Connecticut College in New London, Connecticut. Ohio was much too far away for a weekend trip, then, and I could easily travel to Rockport by train. When they asked me back again for the holiday weekend in my sophomore year, I accepted enthusiastically.

Mornings, from our second-floor bedrooms, Aunt Jinnee and I could hear the clunks and creaks upstairs as George got out of bed and dressed. When he thudded down the wooden stairs from the third floor, I knew without having to check my travel clock that it was seven-thirty.

"Good morning," he called to Jinnee as he passed by on his way down.

It was Thanksgiving. Everyone would arrive at four-thirty. Jinnee had been awake since five o'clock when, as usual, she had gone down to the kitchen to make coffee and then returned upstairs to drink a mug in bed. More than two hours later, I pictured her propped with pillows, finishing off the cold cup, leaning back, and looking out the window at the November-bleak yard. The apple tree was bare, and the cloudy sky threatened snow.

George opened the bathroom door and thundered down the steep stairs to the kitchen. Jinnee gently shooed the big black Newfoundland, Kippy, from the end of her bed, and Zaidee, the Siamese cat, from under the covers. Kippy padded into the third bedroom to wake their younger son, my cousin Mike, and Jean-Luc, his business school friend, a charming Frenchman.

I could hear George downstairs in the kitchen, shaking the iron grating and rattling coal into the cast iron stove that heated the room, waving Zaidee off the warming ledge. George was frying bacon, toasting a piece of housekeeper Aili's whole-wheat bread, and reheating the big pot of five o'clock coffee on the stovetop's gas rings while waiting for water to boil for his precisely timed three-minute egg.

Every morning, with a quick flick of a knife, George would expertly slice off the top and spoon out morsels of soft yolk and firmer white from the inside, leaving the pristine shell in the cup. When he finished eating his toast, he would stand to pour himself a second cup of coffee, then sit down again at the wooden table. Slowly, he would unwrap the cellophane from a small, narrow cigar, which he lit with a single deft stroke of wooden match against box, then puff meditatively, staring out the kitchen windows. The windows framed his small garden, the bird feeder, and the meadow stretching from the house all the way to the road.

Now awake and dressed, I came downstairs and into the kitchen. George wondered out loud whether Ketchopoulous's Market still had good squash. There were many things to be done today before everyone arrived, he reminded me. Standing by the windows, I could see four sheep huddled by the fence.

Jinnee arrived in her long blue bathrobe with quilted lapels, a cigarette in one hand and her empty mug in the other. In the robe's pockets, she usually stowed a couple of half-full packs of Pall-Malls, an extra cigarette holder, and the butane lighter Mike had given her for her birthday, along with some Kleenex and a carbon drawing pencil. She had swept her long hair away from her striking oval face and fastened it on each side with a small comb. Her deep-set blue-green eyes, high cheekbones, and straight nose reminded me of my mother.

"Aren't you going to eat anything?" George puffed.

"Nope."

"All right. Do what you want. It's your life, you know. But you'll be sick again."

This scene has remained with me all these years. George was still slowly but audibly exhaling fragrant cigar smoke while Jinnee poured a cup of steaming coffee from the bottomless pot on the stove. She set the cup on the table and, scanning the corner shelves by the door, went over to extract a small slate and a narrow stylus from among stacks of earthenware bowls and pitchers, a barometer, two small African statues, a Bavarian nutcracker, and a copy of the 1962 *Farmer's Almanac*. She returned to the table and sat down, stubbed out her cigarette in George's ashtray and replaced it in the short holder with another, lit the new one, inhaled, and looked over her to-do list written on the slate.

"We'll have to get Donny over here to separate that ram from the ewes," George was saying. "Look at the way he's butting them. He aims right for their kidneys. He's no good. No good. We'll sell him in the spring." He puffed slowly. "Do you need anything at the market? I'm going to have a talk with Ketchopoulous about some good squash."

He turned toward me: "I talk to him in Greek, don't you know. Oh, yes, the whole family is working there—four sons and a daughter. As soon as they get to be old enough, then *wooops*! They're working for the old man. The Greeks are the best businessmen in the world, you know. The whole family is over there, talking in Greek, and they know I understand it. But the other day I heard one of them—one of the boys—call his sister something that wasn't exactly nice, so I told him, 'Never say that again about a lady in my presence.' In Greek, though. You wouldn't understand it if I said it in Greek. And he said, like this, you know,"—George simpered—"'Yes, Mr. Demetrios, sir.'

"Oh, they're clever all right, but they'll never be anything but grocery clerks. But rich. Oh, we can't forget that. Rich.

"Jinnee, do you need anything or do you not?" He puffed. "Well, I can't sit here all day, you know."

"Everything's all ready," Jinnee assured him. "The turkey is ready for the oven, and Aili baked two loaves of bread yesterday. We're having your good corn and beans from the garden we put in the freezer last summer. And Hilja is bringing three pies. I just have to count up the number of people—there's Ross and Hilja with Sandy and Ritchie, then Christine with Billy, and our old friend Molly, and Mike and that nice Jean-Luc, and the three of us. Twelve. We'll have to move more chairs out to the barn and get Mike and his friend to put leaves in the table."

George: "If you can get him out of bed. Oh, I know, he needs his rest on vacation. But that boy never gets *up* before two o'clock unless we drag him out of bed."

Jinnee: "Now, George, he works very hard, and you should be proud of what he's done at school. You always pick on him for these silly things like sleeping late. Why don't you give him any praise? You should be happy he can be home for holidays."

George: "I don't see him working very hard or getting good marks."

"Good morning, Jinnee," I interjected, moving from beside the window to give her a quick kiss.

"Aren't you going to give me a kiss too?" said George.

I leaned over to kiss George's lined cheek. He put his arm around my shoulder.

"Ah, haven't you got any boyfriends? You need a little loving, yes? If I were young, you know, I'd show her a thing or two." He winked at Jinnee.

"She has time, George," Jinnee said.

I smiled and attempted to move toward the fridge, but George gently held my arm.

"Now, when I was young and handsome—well, I still am, but I was even better looking then—before I came back to the United States, when I was at the Beaux-Arts in Paris, we had a crowd of students, we were all great friends. Frenchmen and Jews, a German girl, Greeks. We used to pose for each other, give each other food. It was a wild crowd in many ways, you know, very free, except for me, because I always thought it was important not to be wild in some ways. You remember this, you wait until you find the one you love until you give yourself away."

"Now, George," Jinnee said.

"Just a minute here, Jinnee. I never kissed a girl, not once during that time. Well, I mean I had just so much time. I kept working every minute, don't you know. Well, I waited until I came here, to Boston, and your aunt was one of my students. I was old by that time. Well, not too old. And she was a young, sweet girl. A good artist, by the way. Of course, she needed me to teach her exactly how to draw."

"Now, George.…"

"*Will* you keep quiet, Jinnee! For *God's* sake! This is my story. Ah, you Burtons are all alike, always want to have the spotlight. Well, do you mind if I continue now? Do I have your permission, your highness?"

To me: "You have the same eyes as your Aunt Virginia, by the way. Wonderful eyes, like a cat. Shows spirit in a woman. But you have to know how to use them. Now… Oh, yes. Of course, I had to teach Jinnee how to draw. She makes more than I do now, by the way, from those books of hers. But I keep her around because she's a good cook. It takes the spirit of an artist to be a good cook.

"But now, I will continue. In Paris, one of these friends of mine, who was a wild fellow like the others, went with me one night to an ice cream parlor, and as we were sitting there, we watched these young boys come in with their young girlfriends, pretty, you know, with pink cheeks and full skirts and little waists. We watched them buying sodas and ice cream cones, and smiling at each other, and this friend said to me, 'George,'—in French, by the way, for I spoke French better then than I speak English now—he said, 'You know, George, I wish that I had come just once with a young girl to buy an ice cream soda when I was young and innocent.' Isn't that something? It's really marvelous, you see, because he had spent his youth working, he was a good artist, and fell in with this wild group of people—*les bohèmes* we call them— and *he* wanted to be young and buy ice cream for a young girl with a ponytail. Well, of course, it was impossible.

"You work hard now, but you have fun, too. Have lots of boyfriends if you like, but wait till you settle for just one. And besides, I'll always wait for you. But remember this from me: don't ever play games with a boy unless you are sure he knows it's a game too. Will you remember that from me?"

I had learned not to interrupt George's monologues with expressions of my own opinion, not even to agree. Now, though, he seemed to have concluded his story, and I nodded yes.

"Now you remember that."

⁂

I moved toward the counter and cut some slices from the square homemade loaf to make toast, then got the pitcher of orange juice from the refrigerator as Jinnee began to take George's dishes from the table.

"Can't you keep *still*, you two, when I'm talking? Well, I can't stay here all day. I'm a busy man, don't you know."

He went to the closet for his overcoat, pulled a black beret from its pocket, and, positioning it low on his forehead, stood ready to open the door.

"You like a little *vino* for dinner? Yes? Oh, I know how you like wine. We are going to have the best. You're sure you don't need anything, Jinnee? Okay. See you later."

He saluted and ushered Kippy out the door. We watched him walk toward the garage. He got into the little white Peugeot and put it in reverse, backed out from the garage, then lurched forward along the driveway. He drove past the woodpile, the sheep meadow, the mailbox. Finally, he turned right onto Washington Street toward Rockport.

⁂

"He'll probably never learn how to drive that car," Jinnee murmured as I buttered my toast, poured juice and coffee, and sat down.

"Would you like some scrambled eggs?" she said.

"No, thanks. I'll eat this afternoon. You know, Aili was going to teach me how to do a dropped egg, but I ruined three and gave up. I haven't learned how to bake the bread, either, but I did manage a batch of chocolate-chip cookies. We ate most of them before they cooled. Will she be here over the weekend?" I asked.

"No, she's spending Thanksgiving with her niece in Marblehead. That means we all have to get the dishes done tonight so there'll be some for breakfast tomorrow."

"Wine with dinner makes you not mind washing dishes afterward. Maybe we'll have a session like last year's, when we had rock 'n' roll on the radio and Mike was throwing the dishes to us to dry after he washed them," I said.

"It better not be like that," Jinnee replied. "But remember our neighbor Molly? Eighty-six and doing the twist? She's been coming for years now. She wouldn't miss our Thanksgiving for anything. We'll have to get Mike and Jean-Luc to put the leaves in the table and take enough chairs out to the barn."

I finished my toast and coffee and quickly rinsed the dishes in the sink.

"I thought I might walk Kippy out to the Point," I said, pulling on a heavy sweater and my knit hat. "Do you want to come? Or do you want me to take stuff out to the barn now?"

"Maybe you could take these nuts and wooden bowls out and straighten things up. We'll take all the dishes and set the table after the boys get it arranged. I don't think I'll go out to the Point. I haven't been feeling well lately, and Mike brought me some new mystery stories—I'm in the middle of one now."

"Okay. I'll go and clean up a little," I said, though to my mind the thirty years' creative work in Jinnee's studio didn't need cleaning up. It inspired me. I felt grateful to be sharing this time and place with these remarkable people.

⚜

I pushed the TV aside, pulled a heavy oval oak table into the center of the space, and placed the bowls of nuts on an old wooden chest. Kippy was scratching at the door. The big black dog and I left the barn and started off for Folly Point. The day was chilly, damp, and gray—a typical Massachusetts Thanksgiving. I trailed Kippy up the drive, past the house, George's garden, and the bare, dry grapevines still clinging to wires strung between granite posts near the garage.

Through the bare limbs of trees, I could glimpse the Atlantic, mostly hidden in leafy summertime, as I walked toward Washington Street.

I would turn left onto the paved road and, a few yards farther on, bear right onto the lane leading to Folly Point. But just then, the white Peugeot veered into the driveway, and George slowed and waved.

Leaning across the front seat to roll down the passenger side window as he braked, he called "Halloo! Working up an appetite? Okay. Okay. Have a good time, but don't be too long. There's a lot to do here. People coming soon, you know."

The car lurched past me toward the garage.

Thanksgiving 1962 Notes

An interest in the subject, something you want to say definitely about the subject, this is the first condition of a portrait: Henri, *The Art Spirit*, page 20.

When I was at the Beaux-Arts in Paris: L'école nationale supérieure des Beaux-Arts. As a student, George also attended the Sorbonne in Paris and the Pennsylvania School of Fine Arts in Philadelphia. He had emigrated from Macedonia at the age of fifteen and arrived in Boston, where he had first earned his living as a dishwasher and shoeshine boy. His sketches, done between jobs, revealed his charm and talent, and through a sponsor, he was offered a job at a Boston newspaper. He enrolled in art school, funded by a wealthy mentor, and soon developed into a promising sculptor. His 1947 book, *When Greek Meets Greek* (Houghton Mifflin Company), with drawings by the author, showcases George's engaging, storytelling charisma.

Aili was going to teach me how to do a dropped egg: Aili Runsala was the Demetrios family's neighbor and housekeeper.

Virginia Lee Demetrios (1909–1968), *A Rose Is a Rose*, undated, linoleum block print. Collection of the Cape Ann Museum, Gloucester, MA.

CHAPTER FIVE

Summer 1963

Go on anyway. Everything depends on those who go on anyway.

I WAS EAGER TO SPEND A WHOLE SUMMER AT FOLLY COVE WITH JINNEE and George. Although I don't remember exactly how the idea originated or how the plan developed (I don't believe I invited myself, but I may have), I arrived toward the end of June.

My bedroom window, curtained with Jinnee's block-printed *A Rose is a Rose* pattern, framed a view of the old apple tree and the spot where the neighborhood party had taken place on my first day, when I'd felt so awkward. Nights, as I turned over in bed to stare at the crack of light under the bedroom door, I took stock of my surroundings. I was keeping stray notes and a journal to jot down conversations and descriptions so that years later I'd remember this singular world.

Stored in my corner closet, I found an extra bedspread, some photographs, an old car seat, and an extra roll of toilet paper. Opposite, near my bed, stood a wide, dark, wooden bookcase filled with paperbacks and stacks of old *Life* magazines and *New Yorkers* with many cartoons cut out. Next to that, a skinny bookcase, with Rainer Maria Rilke's *Letters to a Young Poet,* John Updike's *Rabbit Run,* and some big art books for summer browsing.

The old wooden dresser was painted white: there I set a photo of my mother in a plain frame, and on the big matching mirror I taped a New Yorker cartoon—a man in a bathing suit and sunglasses on a beach blanket, lying on the sand inside an hourglass, summertime slipping away. On a scrap of paper, I also affixed a quote from Robert Henri's book *The Art Spirit* to remind me that *"Art…is simply a question of doing things, anything well. It is not an outside, extra thing."*

I loved the small, battered rolltop desk across the room with its half-scraped-off Red Sox decal on the center drawer. (Had it been Aris's? Mike's?) Inside, pigeonhole slots contained a blue blotter, scissors, India ink and worn pencils, a penny bank, a hula girl statuette, and a broken clock. On the lower shelf of the bedside table, I found an Army flashlight, some old coins, and a plastic memo book.

⸎

My cousin Aris, who'd been visiting for a few days with his wife and young son, drove me to Rockport for my first day on the job at a bookstore and offered a warm-hearted wish "for a beautiful summer" as he said goodbye.

With Aris and Mike now adults, maybe Jinnee and George welcomed me as a summer boarder to enliven their empty nest. And, too, Jinnee may have been moved to repay my grandfather's long-ago generosity. When Jeanne D'Orge left Alfred Burton and their children to live with her lover and devote herself to art, my grandparents had welcomed Jinnee's older sister Christine, who was then in her late teens, to their Cleveland home. She lived with them for some time before moving to New York to begin a stage career. Virginia Lee, at sixteen, stayed with a California school friend's family until she finished high school and won a scholarship to art school in San Francisco before later joining her father in Boston.

Ross, the youngest of the siblings, attended various boarding schools. Returning from Army service in the '40s, Ross came to Cape Ann to live near Jinnee in Lanesville, where he met and married Hilja Johnson. Their two sons, Sandy and Ritchie, were, like Aris and Mike, my second cousins. Ross and Hilja both joined the Folly Cove Designers, and in 1953, Ross, a silversmith, opened Burton's Silver Shop on Bearskin Neck, Rockport's walking street full of small shops, restaurants, and souvenir stands.

I think it was Ross, with his connections in town, who arranged my job at the bookstore owned by the widowed Mrs. Dangerfield.

The Mariner's Bookstall was located in a two-story wooden building near the intersection of Mt. Pleasant Street and Broadway, around the corner from T-Wharf. Jinnee and George dusted off their tan 1949 Dodge roadster for my commute of a few miles from Folly Cove to Rockport. We agreed I'd pay for gas.

⸙

I loved Rockport. In the early morning, the grassy island at the junction of Mt. Pleasant and Broadway was deeply shaded. Leafy branches rustled in a light breeze. Across the street from the bookstore, the Chamber of Commerce information booth opened early, its staff fielding questions and handing out maps. On park benches, old men read newspapers and women with baby carriages knitted tiny garments. By late morning, the corner became bright and sunny, crowded with tourists' cars and boys on motor scooters. Families carried sailing gear to the modest, gray-shingled Sandy Bay Yacht Club at the end of T-Wharf. Narrow alleyways and gaps between the old wooden stores along Mt. Pleasant Street revealed glimpses of rocky shore and the ocean beyond. Each vista was fractured into seascapes painted on easels set up on side streets and beaches by an army of amateur *plein-air* artists.

⸙

During slow hours at the bookshop, I read Rachel Carson's recently published *Silent Spring*. I took home advance copies of debut novels like *The Collector* by John Fowles and *V* by Thomas Pynchon. I was educating myself in this new place with its unfamiliar people. I read and read, and began to believe that by pursuing my own way, I might accomplish something exciting and meaningful, whatever that might turn out to be. But to begin with, I didn't know what "my own way" was: as an eldest daughter, I was sensitized to what was expected of me and how I would be judged by others, mainly adults. I was cautious. I seldom acted according to my own desires and goals and often was too unaware even to define what they were. Spontaneity was not my strong point.

At the back of the store, between the children's books and broom closet, was a window: beyond the crumbling breakwall a mile offshore, white sails and lobster boats dotted the blue Atlantic. Close in, at the Yacht Club, sailboats rocked at their moorings. In the middle distance in the inner harbor, skiffs and fishing boats bobbed near Rockport's iconic red fishing shack, the picturesque Motif #1, decked out with lobster buoys.

"It's a beautiful day," I might report to Mrs. Dangerfield, over my shoulder. "The wind is picking up, and there are a couple of Star boats on the bay."

At that, she might look up from her day's reading, a new book she had chosen, its cover protected with a piece of the store's brown wrapping paper.

"Some people can enjoy beach days and some must remember their jobs. Business will probably be slow all day today, except for customers like those two women in wet bathing suits who were in yesterday. Came in and dripped water all over the floor, then bought a thirty-five-cent mystery story.

"Sometimes I don't know where I get the strength to go on. Business comes in waves. A store like this one can't carry every-thing—there simply isn't enough room. Those paperbacks hardly pay for themselves, and I never know whether I'll break even on an order or not."

It was true that business was not booming. I understood that Mrs. D was concerned about finances. It affected her mood. She seemed annoyed when I gazed out that back window. She pointed out that I chatted too freely with customers who came in to browse. And I confess that an occasional young "customer"—usually a Bill, or Henry, or Tim—might stop in to pass the time or casually arrange a date.

"Let's picnic at lunchtime," Henry might say. "I'll meet you at noon, and we'll ride bikes to the Headlands."

"Henry is still sowing his wild oats" Mrs. D cautioned me. "But his family is well established in Boston. They have a lovely home here in the summer. Another family used to rent that house. I'm glad *that* boy hasn't been in here after you like he was last summer when Alice was helping me. This summer, they've rented an old house in East Gloucester."

⚜

By late July, Mrs. Dangerfield was showing an unfriendliness I couldn't comprehend: I arrived on time, finished the tasks she set, and tried to be pleasant. Often she left me alone to dust, sweep, make phone calls, or deposit bank receipts and lock up at the end of the day. As I reflect on it now, she may have been deeply unhappy. It seems probable she was frustrated by her situation; then too, I can't rule out a dislike for me personally. She never fired me but made known that she considered me immature and self-centered. In any case, by mid-August, Mrs. Dangerfield was hinting that she no longer needed my help. I didn't know how to respond. Her baffling passive-aggressiveness embarrassed me.

Uncle Ross advised me that I'd best resign. So, after dinner on August 16, with Jinnee at my elbow for moral support, I phoned Mrs. Dangerfield at home and told her I could no longer work there. Her response was abrupt and frosty. The next afternoon, after a busy day alone in the bookshop, I closed the wooden screen door behind me for the last time.

In my journal, I noted, "It's a shame everything was so hidden and nothing was said…but at least after tomorrow I'm free."

It seemed best, then, to step back and think about how to spend the remaining precious weeks of summer. I'd be able to concentrate on the design lessons Jinnee offered and attend George's challenging drawing class every day.

⚜

Summer 1963 Notes

Go on anyway. Everything depends on those who go on anyway: Henri, *The Art Spirit*, page 214.

I taped a New Yorker cartoon: drawn by artist Fernando Krahn, published in the *New Yorker* magazine, July 20, 1963.

Art is simply a question: Henri, *The Art Spirit*, page 15.

Virginia Lee Demetrios (1909–1968), *Grass*, undated, linoleum block print. Collection of the Cape Ann Museum, Gloucester, MA.

CHAPTER SIX

Life Drawing

The grip of the line. Note how a line takes hold. It hooks the vital parts together.

I BEGAN ATTENDING GEORGE'S DAILY LIFE DRAWING CLASS AT THE large Woodbury Street studio he inherited from his mentor and professor, the sculptor Charles Grafly. George himself was a popular, even legendary, teacher.

To get there, I followed the winding uphill path across the stream and through the woods behind the house. One morning I arrived late, breathless and a little sweaty. I hurried up the studio's stairs and carefully opened the wooden screen door, then closed it quietly behind me. Inside, I walked down three steps, grabbed two drawing pencils, a sheaf of blank newsprint, and an eraser from the battered table in the corner, picked up an easel from the stack, and carried it to an empty chair in the circle of waiting students. Glancing at me, George nodded curtly.

"It's late now, so we'll start," George was saying in his accented English. "When I was a student, we posed for each other when there was no model. We'll do some quick ones. Vicky, take off your shoes and model for us."

Vicky stepped up to the platform in the center of the circle of chairs. She crouched low, barefoot, wearing a turquoise skirt and yellow jersey.

George lingered behind Pat's chair. He kept an eye on her hands.

"Don't be so slow!" he said to her. "Look at me, a hundred years old and I have more energy than you!"

He took the lap easel, motioned her out of her chair, sat down, and ripped her cautious drawing from the metal clips fastened to the board. He took a sharpened carbon pencil out of his khaki work-shirt pocket.

"Watch me," he said. "See the shape of the skirt for the shape of the top. It's really quite wonderful, don't you know!"

I adjusted my own easel's single leg so the board rested on my knees, then clipped my wad of blank newsprint vertically and began to trace the lines of Vicky's body. Now she was standing, arms outstretched in the dim morning light. Vicky broke the pose and stepped down from the platform.

"Good girl!" George said. "Susie next."

Susie kicked off her sandals and took a position. The quick tearing of sketches punctuated each change of pose. The floor was soon littered.

"*Where* is that model? That crazy Louise!" George patrolled our ring of chairs, taking a small cigar out of the slim packet in his pocket. He studied it a moment before slipping off its wrapper, striking a match, and lighting it. Puffing pensively, he arrived behind Davis's easel.

"You can't *make* a hand, you know," he said, relishing the cigar. "You can only draw the shapes and sizes you see. Draw the *shapes*, the *shapes*. Draw the relative sizes, and the picture will make itself."

From across the circle, I peered over my board.

"*Bah!* Don't start with line drawings! Get the *shapes!* Get the shapes of the spaces *between* the shapes. You must learn to see, to judge with your eyes!"

He covered Davis's hand with his own and energetically moved the pencil in large sweeps.

"*All over the place! All over the place!* The first rule is to *fill the paper!*"

He straightened and challenged Davis with shrewd brown eyes.

"*Come* now! You know the first rule?" he demanded.

"Fill the paper," Davis responded.

"*That's right!*" George said, tearing off the scribble he had made of Davis's last drawing. "Now get to *work!*"

He continued his tour.

"*Faster, faster,*" George scolded. "Don't be so timid. *All over the place!*"

He glanced at the student model.

"That's enough, Elizabeth. Now try one like this." He demonstrated, curving his whole body forward.

George Demetrios (1896–1974), untitled (nude woman with outstretched knee), mid-twentieth century, charcoal on paper. Collection of the Cape Ann Museum, Gloucester, MA. Gift of Riverrun LLC, 2017 (2017.052.3).

"*No?* All right, all right. Do what you want. Oh, *baby,* that's good. Now, can everybody see?"

"We had the back the last time," Richard reminded him.

George slowly turned the model's lazy-Susan platform halfway, so Richard had a forward-facing view.

"All *right.* Is everybody satisfied *now? Let's go!*"

Just then, Louise entered. Silently, we watched her descend the three stairs. She was wearing a white peasant blouse and yellow cotton skirt, a broad-brimmed straw gardening hat, sunglasses, and high-heeled, open-toed red shoes. She carried a matching red patent leather pocketbook.

"All right, Louise. Hurry up," George said dryly.

Louise went into the back room to undress.

Elizabeth left the platform. The floor was already ankle-deep in scrapped sketches. I pushed my legs and arms out straight in front of me: my bare feet were dirty. I arched backward and brushed the hair off my face, then noticed that my hands were black with carbon pencil. Dust motes swirled in the sunlight as the studio brightened. I gathered up a batch of my own discards—the figures looked stiff and awkward.

Louise emerged, took off her blue smock and, naked, stepped onto the platform. George was slowly removing the cellophane from a fresh cigarillo. He spoke softly, for maximum effect.

"*Your* job is to model for us, Louise. *Our* job is to draw. My name is George Demetrios, and I am proud of it. I think I am an artist, and I work as hard as I can to do the best I can do. *You* must try just as hard to pose well. The jobs have to be done, and we must concentrate on the jobs, not on ourselves."

He lit the cigarillo.

"All right, now. Let's have a good one, Louise."

On the platform, a model's nude body becomes an object— just a fact. But when George addressed Louise directly, her naked-ness suddenly seemed bizarre, her body ugly—long and bony and angular. She had bushy red hair and freckles everywhere.

She began by lying down, so we repositioned our paper horizon-tally. George continued his circuit, leaning over our shoulders to comment. Louise began changing poses more quickly, and we were seeing and drawing faster, sensing the forms and grasping the whole.

"All right, Louise, try something else. Let's get some *life* into this one," George chided. "That's better."

He stopped behind Jean.

"That's really very wonderful, you know! You have a real feeling. But get the foot back, higher on the paper. You have it sticking out of her shoulder!"

George moved on.

"Mrs. Morris! What is closest to you goes at the *bottom* of the paper. Which is closer, that *foot* or *that leg*? If your nose grew long, which would it touch first? Look at my big Greek nose. It's growing. Look where it touches first!" George held a pencil to the end of his nose and walked toward Louise until the point touched her foot.

"Do you see *now*?" he said.

"I think so," said Mrs. Morris.

"*Mrs. Morris*! We are not here to *think*," George said. "*Godammit! Excuse me, Mrs. Morris, but *draw*!"

Exasperated, or pretending to be, he turned away.

Louise stood up.

"You are tired? I'm tired too." Gesturing toward the dressing room, he said, "Louise, I want to talk to you."

Then to the class: "We'll take a break. Change your places in the room and get different-sized paper. We'll have some longer poses in a minute."

During the pause, I looked through my throwaways again. Nudes were harder to draw, but these last rapid sketches seemed better. Standing up, I took a stack of the larger paper from the table and chose a chair on the opposite side of the circle. Davis sat down beside me. The others began to take their places. George returned.

"*Louise!*" he called.

Louise stubbed out her cigarette and took off her blue smock.

"Hold these as long as you can," George told her.

Eyes flicked from model to paper, squinting. First, the big shapes, the line of action. Then the smaller forms. Get the head down. The space between the arms. How big? Where's the hand? Rough sketches blossomed and fell.

George stopped behind me: "Don't be so lady-like! *All over the place*!"

Then, "What's the first rule?"

"Fill the paper," I recited.

George took my easel.

"Get up," he said, taking my seat. He nodded to Davis as he began drawing. "You watch this too. *All over the place*! I don't know anything. I can't make anything! *Watch* now, you two! Here's the foot, there are the arms. Fill the paper. *Fast, fast*! Don't try to be an intellectual. Draw what you see! Over *here*! Up *there*! This for that. The size of the ankle for the size of the wrist. The space between the legs. Get the shapes. Get the relative sizes. The hand for the head. You can't make it yourself. All the relations are there, you just have to see them. *Faster.* Catch it in a moment. Your lines must be strong. You must know what you see. You must know what you like. Once you get that, *then* you can get the details. The eyelashes, if you like. The fingernails. *Now.* Let's see what you can do."

He handed over the easel and stood up. I sat.

"And don't sit too close! You get a better perspective farther away. See the whole thing! The ensemble. See the relative values. *Everything fits together*. Be strong. Get the feeling; get inside what you are trying to do. Like life, don't you know? See what's important! Then go after it."

He bent over my shoulder, breathing audibly and smelling of cigars, his shock of white hair and lined face close to mine.

"Better already," he said. "Now try it again. And get that arm. It's closer than you have it, don't you know."

He moved on. Louise stood. She knelt. She crouched. She was lying again on her side. The strong summer sunlight now brought everything into focus: Louise's pale, freckled skin, the intent faces of the students, the big dusty barn space surrounding our tight circle of chairs. It was nearly noon.

"One more minute, Louise. That's enough," George decided. "Thank you!"

Eyes dry, shoulders tense, I yawned and stretched, stood and stretched again, almost out of breath after expending so much focused energy. Stiffly, I returned my pencils to the table and stacked the chair and easel in the corner. Scooping up armloads of sketches from the floor, I stuffed a morning's hard work into the overflowing wastebaskets, rescuing only a few of the drawings scattered at my feet—a couple of Davis's fluid ones and some of my own earnest efforts.

Sketches in hand, I left the studio alone, feeling released into the world, open to *SEEING* the world as it *IS*, with all the relationships connected—by lines or the spaces between the lines. I moved quickly toward home, down the cool path through the woods, noticing that flies had found fresh raccoon droppings near my feet. In the foreground under a luminous sky, I spotted the house and barn, caught a glimpse of the apple tree, the sheep meadow, the road, and beyond them, out of sight, I imagined the immense ocean and a boundless future.

Life Drawing Notes

The grip of the line. Note how a line takes hold. It hooks the vital parts together: Henri, *The Art Spirit*, page 192.

Virginia Lee Demetrios (1909–1968), *Zaidee and her Kittens*,
undated, ink on linen, linoleum block print. Collection
of the Cape Ann Museum, Gloucester, MA.

CHAPTER SEVEN

Jinnee's Designs

Art in the community has a subtle, unconscious, refining influence.

At first, I found little similarity between George's sponta-neous, spare line drawings and Jinnee's structured, detailed Folly Cove prints. Aris identified his parents' fundamental artistic common ground: the principle of proportional relationships, the harmony of the whole and its parts.

"Both of them taught you how to see.… You saw the world more clearly and more deeply.… You saw connections with things you never saw before. You learned to look at the big stuff and then you went down into detail. All of Jinnee's designs [represent] the same thing. Always the big thing into which the little thing fits.…

"Although my mother and father really were contentious with each other, [when it came to talking] about *art*…they were as one."

He related Jinnee's two additional guidelines: "If you want to make something different from something else, then really make it differ-ent—make it at least twice as big or twice as small, don't fiddle around with the middle stuff because then things will look too much alike."

And, "Whatever you do, do it well!… Once isn't enough.… And play! Turn things around and upside down and backwards."

One striking example is Jinnee's popular Folly Cove design *Zaidee and her Kittens*. Jinnee's elegant Siamese cat and a dark, nameless male regularly managed to produce exponentially multiplying generations. Their progeny revealed a gamut of genetic variations in color and markings, black and white, striped and spotted. (Working on a single linoleum block, Jinnee spent five months just carving tiny dots on Zaidee's fur.)

This humorous design demonstrates Jinnee's skillful uses of dark and light and small to large to comment on these cats' astonishing fertility. The fine quality of the workmanship, down to the tiny "leaves" in the topmost reaches of the cat family tree, the design's pleasing symmetry, its rhythm, and progression combine to make it one of Jinnee's most sought after.

To encourage kitten adoptions, she would offer free sets of *Zaidee* placemats with each new litter. Jinnee lamented how hard it was to keep up with demand for that particular Folly Cove Designers product.

꧁

My mother set the dinner table with a variety of Folly Cove Designers placemats, runners, and tablecloths. As a child, I'd loved them but knew little about the group's origins and mission and next to nothing about block-printing techniques.

Jinnee described her early design classes to Harold in a 1941 letter, penned on brand-new Folly Cove Designers stationery:

> The Folly Cove Designers are a group of people here—year round residents and almost all Finnish—whom I have taught design—I was trying out this theory of mine and found that it worked—worked so well I have now retired from teaching to become a member. It is a cooperative group—we are beginning slowly but gradually we are building up an interest in our work. It is mostly hand-blocking designs on materials and making them into usable things—we have sold a lot and now we are going quite commercial. We have exhibited quite a bit as a group. And some stores in Boston carry our things. I am not so interested in the commercial side as the others. It's the Design that I like—It is original all of it—I start them out with just dots—comparative sizes—every step they take they know why—
>
> Then for ideas they go directly to Nature and select—
>
> I must stop or I'll be giving a design lesson—I'm always doing it before I know it—sometime I shall do a book on it—

OLLY COVE DESIGNERS

OLLY COVE, GLOUCESTER, MASSACHUSETTS

2

I am not so interested in the
commercial side as the others.
It's the Design that I like —
It is original all of it — I start
them out with just dots —
comparative sizes — . Every step
they take they know why —

Then for ideas they go directly
to Nature and select —

I must stop or I'll be giving
a Design lesson — I'm always
doing it before I know it —
Sometime I shall do a book
on it — with very few words too

Letter from Virginia Lee Burton to Harold Hitz Burton,
October 30, 1941 Collection of the author.

with very few words too—It's an accumulation of many ideas and theories; I have just sorted them and arranged the facts so anyone can understand—who wants to.

⁓

The Designers began not as an art class or a women's collective, but as an inclusive community activity. The group's communal spirit has been compared to medieval craftsmen's guilds. Women and men with a common purpose came together to form a cooperative association. They met regularly yet worked independently. If not for Jinnee's passion and motivation, the group might not have thrived over three decades. Inspired by her magnetic leadership and guided by her artistic vision, each member aimed to complete at least one original linoleum block template every year and to carry out every step in the process—designing, drawing, carving, printing, and marketing their projects.

⁓

In 1939, Jinnee's first group exercises began with painting lines, dots, and shapes with a brush—"quite primitive" according to her neighbor Aino Clarke—in order to examine the relationships between a design's black-and-white areas. As individual members became more proficient, their homework became more complex. Jinnee devised intricate exercises for them and required students to follow a set of prescribed assignments with disciplined, almost mathematical, precision.

A 1982 retrospective Cape Ann Historical Association catalog described the system:

> Working within a sequence of five sizes and tonal gradations, the forms were arranged to display the relationship between them and the pattern as a whole…. A subject or motif…was drawn in five tones ranging from white to gray to solid black, against backgrounds whose tones followed the same sequence of gradations until all possible combinations were exhausted.
>
> Next, substituting size as a variable, the sequence was repeated. Finally, the subject was arrayed in patterns of circles,

squares, rectangles, then vertically, diagonally, and horizontally within those shapes, until the designer could manipulate the motif as a purely decorative element…. Those carefully structured exercises helped each artist anticipate how a completed design might look when all its elements were in place.

Jinnee described her method as practical and hands-on. She was "a doer, not a thinker," she maintained. Yet, neither Jinnee's work nor the products of other Folly Cove designers should be thought of as folk art, a term often used to indicate handicrafts or paintings by untutored artisans. Public recognition of the professional quality of their work came in the form of invitations to exhibit in museum shows and juried crafts events. In the '40s, New York City's Lord and Taylor department store and a dozen more across the country featured Folly Cove designs in their sidewalk show windows.

Eino Natti working with the Acorn Press. Photograph by Mr. Miller of Rochester, NY. From the Folly Cove Designers Collection of the Cape Ann Museum Library & Archives, Gloucester, MA.

During my summer stay, I developed respect not only for designers' creativity and discipline, but also for their physical strength. To
prepare a linoleum-covered block, twelve by eighteen inches, you first
roughed its surface with fine sandpaper. Next, you applied white shoe
polish or soluble paint as a ground for the design, which you drew with
a brush and black India ink. In this trial-and-error process, you could
correct mistakes with white ink, and, in case of disaster, you could wipe
the block clean with a wet rag and begin again from scratch.

When the drawing was complete, you were ready to incise the
block, which might take weeks or months, depending on the designer's time and the degree of detail. Meticulously and methodically,
you removed white spaces with a sharp knife, leaving the black areas
raised. When the design was perfectly cut, it was ready for printing.

You squeeze a thick dab of resiny printer's ink onto a plate glass
palette and roll it smooth—back and forth, with a gluey sound—with
a rubber printer's brayer. Very thin layers of ink must be applied
repeatedly to the cut block, or you risk filling in the spaces that must
remain clean. If that happens, you wipe off all the ink with turpen-
tine and begin again.

By 1963, the group had long abandoned the original printing
method, jumping barefoot on an inked block, to transfer a design
to fabric placed on the floor. However, Jinnee's hand printing press
demanded upper body and arm strength and endurance. To exert
pressure on the inked block and transfer the design to cotton fabric,
you leaned in, braced your foot, and pulled the handle across from
the opposite side with two hands. To print a tablecloth required
re-inking and resetting the block just so, adjusting the fabric with
each repeated pull.

Fabrics for placemats, runners, and tablecloths were pre-sized
and fringed. The finished prints were hung on a clothesline to dry,
then sorted for display. Placemats were grouped for sale in sets of
four and tagged with a Folly Cove Designers card, hand-lettered with
the name of the designer and the title of the design.

In July 1954, Jinnee communicated optimistically with her editor at Houghton Mifflin, Paul Brooks, about the book that she'd mentioned in her letter to Harold, to be titled *Design? And How!*

Dear Paul,

　　Your visit has inspired and spurred me on to get right to work on DESIGN AND HOW!!! Now I believe you really want the book and of course I really want to get it done…so I shall practice the first rule in the book, And *Do it! Don't talk about it!*

July 26, 1954

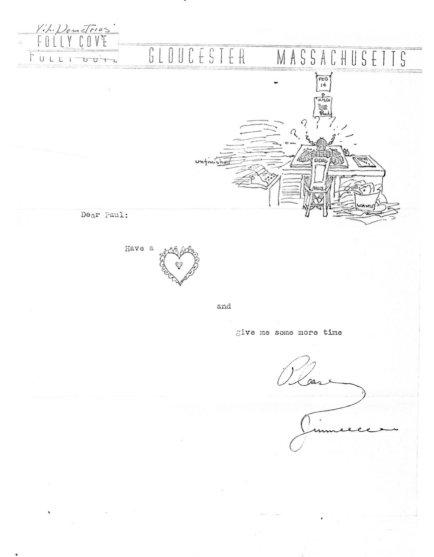

Letters from Virginia Lee Burton to Paul Brooks regarding *Design and How!*, July 26, 1954. From the Virginia Lee Burton Demetrios Collection of the Cape Ann Museum Library & Archives, Gloucester, MA.

A perfectionist, she typed, edited, and retyped page upon page, over and over, trying to simplify and clarify her approach. Yet, despite decades of work, Jinnee never completed her design manual.

⫻

I became curious about the origins of ideas Jinnee told Harold she'd "accumulated, sorted, and arranged" for *Design? And How!* I wanted to understand where the Folly Cove Designers' venture fit into the long history of printed textile design.

Following up on a clue from one former Folly Cove designer, Mary Maletskos, I began to delve into background sources. Mary had suggested in a 1990 interview that when Jinnee was studying at the California School of Fine Arts in 1927, she "apparently did have a real design teacher." Jinnee was then living with the family of her school friend Mabel Holland in Alameda and commuting—by train, ferry boat, and cable car—across the bay to art classes in San Francisco.

"Well, look at this," said Mary in that interview, holding up a copy of the book given to her by Jinnee's friend Mary Greer, a designer herself. "It's exactly what we were doing. And the symbols, then putting it in the lines, and then a border to start with and then to make the border a circle and the overall pattern. Isn't that fascinating? It's just a Folly Cove design, isn't it?… This must have been known by the person who taught [Jinnee]."

I discovered that the book was *A Method for Creative Design* by Adolfo Best-Maugard (1891–1964). When it was published in 1926, Best-Maugard was director general of Drawing and Manual Training for all public schools in Mexico. He had given talks at the University of California, Berkeley, in 1923 and again in 1926, and was familiar with California art schools and the circle of educators in the Bay Area.

Best-Maugard's *Method* focused on seven elements of decorative design inspired by forms in nature and found in traditional Mexican and global folk arts: *point, straight line, spiral, circle, arc, wavy line, S shape, and zigzag.* As Mary Maletskos pointed out, Folly Cove prints offer vivid, original combinations of these same elements, arranging figurative motifs from nature and everyday life as decorative compositions grounded in basic design structures.

Jinnee's conviction that a dedicated beginner can become a competent designer-craftsperson recalls the late nineteenth- and early twentieth-century tradition of the Arts and Crafts movement in England and later in the United States.

In addition to Best-Maugard, I have speculatively identified four other likely artistic influences: William Morris, Walter Crane, Arthur Wesley Dow, and William S. Rice—all educators who, like Jinnee, linked their artistic and pedagogic practice to social ideals.

One indirect forerunner was renowned textile designer William Morris (1834–1895). Multitalented like Jinnee, he was also a painter, entrepreneur, author, and social activist. Morris and his Victorian cohort conceived Arts and Crafts as a social reform movement—a reaction against what they saw as industrialization's harmful, stifling uniformity of products, cruel exploitation of workers, and unconcealed greed. Morris's vision was to restore dignity to labor by elevating the value of well-designed, hand-crafted objects. This influence was tacit: Morris designs were favored by Jinnee's father in furnishings, as evidenced in several sketches of his home.

Walter Crane (1845–1915), a friend and colleague of William Morris, was one of England's most prominent and innovative illustrators of children's books, integrating text and drawings. Jinnee recounted that for birthdays and Christmas, her father presented his children with "beautifully illustrated children's books which he would read aloud." Crane's popular, exquisitely drawn collections of fairy tales and traditional nursery rhymes were almost certainly among her family's "beautifully illustrated" books. As a member of the Arts and Crafts movement, Crane, too, was multitalented: an illustrator, a fine-art painter, a textile printer influenced by Japanese block prints, and also an advocate for social reform through art instruction and practice.

Crane's design theory books, *The Bases of Design* (1898) and *Line and Form* (1900), were originally intended as teaching aids. Some of the ideas from *Line and Form*—for example, the categorization of three basic design elements, line, form, and space—strongly resemble key elements in Jinnee's draft chapters of *Design? And How!*

⬿⬿⬿

Just as Walter Crane's books may have been an early, unconscious influence, the work of renowned American artist, printmaker, and teacher Arthur Wesley Dow (1857–1922) likely had an impact. Dow wrote his influential 1899 book, *Composition: A Series of Exercises in Art Structure for the Use of Students and Teachers*, as a guide to creating visual design. Before he taught at the Art Students' League in New York City, Dow held classes in his own school in Ipswich, Massachusetts, his birthplace, just thirteen miles from Folly Cove. Like Crane, Dow was strongly attracted to Japanese painting and wood-block prints.

And similarly to Crane's book *Line, Form, and Space*, Dow's *Composition* also conceptualized three types of design elements: line, *notan* (a Japanese term translated as light/dark, or mass), and color. Dow's theories emphasized formal relationships over subject matter: no matter what the subject of a print or painting, the ways these three elements related to one another determined its success or failure:

> Composition…expresses the idea upon which the method here presented is founded—the "putting together" of lines, masses and colors to make a harmony…. Composition, building up of harmony, is the fundamental process in all the fine arts…. A natural method is of exercises in progressive order, first building up very simple harmonies…. It offers a means of training for the creative artist, the teacher, or one who studies art for the sake of culture.

⬿⬿⬿

William S. Rice (1873–1963) studied design with one of Dow's West Coast colleagues, Pedro de Lemos. Rice was a student of de Lemos, who was director of the art museum and gallery at Stanford University in Palo Alto. Rice was a wood-block printer, educator, and author associated with the California Arts and Crafts movement. Rice taught drawing and painting and a variety of crafts in the Oakland and Alameda public schools from 1910 to 1943. He exhibited widely in and around San Francisco and was published in the popular *Sunset Magazine*. Jinnee, as a student living in Alameda in 1927, was probably familiar with the block printing of William Rice, Pedro de Lemos, and other well-known California designers, including Best-Maugard, during her formative time in San Francisco. Rice published two books about block printing: *Block Printing in the Schools* (1929) and *Block Prints: How to Make Them* (1941). His work was primarily figurative, though the books also include purely decorative designs using linoleum blocks for printing posters and fabric.

※

It seems likely to me that Jinnee's design concepts and teaching methods devised in the '30s and '40s were influenced by these artists and others. Most certainly, Jinnee's own exceptional artistic imagination was alloyed with idealism and social concerns. All aspects of her art were shaped by her unique personal history: images from her early reading, the Arts and Crafts furnishings in her childhood homes, her father's beautiful draftsman-like drawings and watercolors, her mother's darkly expressive painting and poetry, her brief formal arts education in California, and George's instruction at the Boston Museum School.

Jinnee's cooperative vision and hands-on instruction inspired her neighbors to believe in themselves individually as designer-craftspeople and strengthened bonds within the whole Folly Cove community.

※

Jinnee's Designs Notes

Art in the community has a subtle, unconscious, refining influence: Henri, *The Art Spirit*, page 117.

Both of them taught you how to see: Cape Ann Museum (CAM) Folly Cove Designers Archive Collection A78, box #5, interviews by Bowdoin College Professor Penny Martin: Interview with Aris Demetrios, San Francisco, CA, June 25, 1993. Pages 8 and 20.

Working on a single linoleum block: *Yankee* magazine, September 1957, page 37.

The Folly Cove Designers are a group of people here: letter from VLB to HHB, October 30, 1941.
   To distinguish her design work from her established identity as author/illustrator Virginia Lee Burton, Jinnee used her married name as founder of the Folly Cove Designers, Virginia Lee Demetrios.

Quite primitive: Goodwin, Deborah, in *Folly Cove Designers: A Retrospective*, 1982, Cape Ann Historical Association: "Folly Cove Designers/ Designer-Craftsmen 1938–1969," page 3.

Working within a sequence of five sizes and tonal gradations: ibid., page 4.

To prepare a linoleum block: for a more detailed description, see Natti, Eino, "Folly Cove Block printing," in *Craft Horizons*, Summer 1951, pages 38–39.

Dear Paul: letter from VLB to Paul Brooks, her longtime editor at Houghton Mifflin, July 26, 1954.

Following up on a clue from one former designer: Cape Ann Museum (CAM) Folly Cove Designers Archive Collection A78, box #5, interviews by Professor Penny Martin: Interview with Mary Maletskos, July 6, 1990, Gloucester, MA.

Jinnee was living with her school friend: thanks to Ross (Sandy) Burton for his research and identification of Jinnee's host family.

Given to her by her friend Mary Greer: Mary Greer was born in Cheyenne, Wyoming, in 1895. She studied at the Boston Museum School and in Paris and followed Jinnee and George to Gloucester. Her husband was Donald (Papa) Greer, a close friend to George.

The book was: Best-Maugard, Adolfo, *A Method for Creative Design* (reprint), Dover Publications, 1990. An artist, Best-Maugard had made detailed illustrations of pre-Hispanic excavation findings in the Valley of Mexico earlier in his career, as assistant to anthropologist Franz Boas.

William Morris: Morris, William, *The Art of the People* (1879), *Arts and Crafts* (1909), and many other books, both fiction and non-fiction.

Walter Crane: Crane, Walter, *The Bases of Design* (1898), *Line and Form* (1900). They were based on lectures given in Manchester, England, where he was director of design at the Manchester Municipal School.

Beautifully illustrated children's books: in VLB autobiography, small booklet, 1962, Houghton Mifflin.

Dow's theories emphasized formal relationships: Dow, Arthur, *Composition: A Series of Exercises in Art Structure for the Use of Students and Teachers*, second edition, 1912, University of California

Press reprint, 1997, page 63. As an American Arts and Crafts artist, teacher, and teacher of teachers, Arthur Wesley Dow anticipated abstraction in modern art in theory and practice. His most famous pupils, modernists Max Weber and Georgia O'Keeffe, carried his methods even further into abstraction.

A related book on design is Bothwell, Dorr, and Mayfield, Marlys, *Notan: the Light Dark Principle of Design*, Dover Publications, 1991 (1968). "Notan enables the artist to achieve a Gestalt—or more simply, to create a *design*." Bothwell, like Jinnee, studied at the California School of Fine Arts in the 1920s.

William S. Rice: Rice, William S., *Block Prints: How to Make Them*, second edition, 2019 (1941), Pomegranate Communications, Coventry, UK.

Pedro de Lemos: (1882–1954) author of *The Art Teacher* (1931) on the principles of design applied to various media. Artist in the Arts and Crafts tradition, director of the Stanford University art museum, editor-in-chief of *School Art* magazine from 1919–1950, and president of the Carmel Art Association in the late 1920s.

Margaret "Peggy" Norton (1905–2000), *Baked Bean Supper*, ca. 1954, ink on linen, linoleum block print. Cape Ann Museum, Gloucester, MA.

CHAPTER EIGHT

Neighbors

*When you paint a background you are painting all that volume of
space which is the setting of your subject...the air he breathes....*

A MEMORABLE CAST OF CHARACTERS AND THEIR VIVID PERSONALITIES
remain with me as I look back now on that singular place,
Folly Cove. As a visitor, I was naturally curious and paying attention, noticing in detail the newness of my surroundings.

At the start of my summer stay, I was following certain routines:
curling my hair in rollers at night; dressing on Sunday mornings
and driving the old Dodge to services at the Universalist Church in
Rockport. After a while, though, these habits fell by the wayside as I
became accustomed to George and Jinnee's comfortable, informal
ways. We shared dinner with neighbors several evenings a week at
the wooden kitchen table, talking, laughing, listening to stories, and
drinking more wine than I was used to. Dinners sometimes lasted
well into the night, unlike our six o'clock family sit-downs at home.
Slowly I adapted to a more social existence.

Jinnee and George's friends and colleagues fascinated me.
Though I got to know only a handful of neighbors, how extraordinary they seemed! They were completely *themselves*, each one unfor-
gettable and sometimes surprising, their amusing, likeable, and
even unappealing traits lending color and variety.

A week after my arrival, Jinnee and I drove to Gloucester for a
dance class with her friend and teacher Ina Hahn. Twenty years
younger than Jinnee, Ina—like Jinnee—had spent childhood
in Newton Center, near Boston. She had become a professional
dancer in New York, performing in Broadway musicals and in the

works of renowned modern dance pioneer Doris Humphrey. Ina emanated a sprightly energy. She taught a modified Humphrey-technique dance class, full of quick triplets, generous swirls, and spiraling falls and recoveries.

I'm sure my grandmother had described to Jinnee my own joy in dancing and performing, starting from an early age and continuing through my college years and beyond. And I knew dancing had always been important for Jinnee—she had a graceful, grounded vitality and sturdy Burton legs! We took Ina Hahn's invigorating dance class together with a few others in her small studio, and afterward, we emerged happily sweaty and tired. Our shared passion for moving helped me compensate for my lack of talent for drawing.

On Friday nights, the kitchen windows glowed warmly when George, Jinnee, Folly Cove Designer Eino Natti, and a fourth—often Norman von Rosenvinge, sometimes Fen Lasell—played poker for penny stakes at the kitchen table, smoking cigars or Pall Malls with glasses of whiskey or beer at hand.

I believed myself in a vague, unstable stage of life, dithering between girlhood and womanhood, while the others all were adults. George was in his late sixties then, and Norman and Eino nearer Jinnee's age, about fifty-four. To me, a nineteen-year-old, even my cousin Mike, twenty-eight, seemed out of reach, so much older and more urbane. Aris, at thirty-two, a successful sculptor in a modern vein, was twelve years older than I and twelve years younger than my parents, and seemingly of another generation.

Eino Natti was a founding member of the Folly Cove Designers. Many of his design motifs reflected his connections to the sea, animals, the military, and sports. I especially liked his designs *Yo Heave Ho* (1953), *Ringed Neck Pheasants* (1957), and *Gloucester Harbor* (1961).

Eino was the best of all possible neighbors. His niece Isabel Natti once described him to me as a "love teacher"—a solid, strong, capable man who treated everyone with kindness and respect. He kept a small vegetable garden and made little money. His daily routine, Isabel said, included checking in on a number of people, including his father, whom he helped with chores and errands. Years later, when Isabel Natti owned the Sarah Elizabeth shop in Rockport's Station Square, she printed (on Eino's Acorn press) her own designs in the Folly Cove tradition.

One summer afternoon, as I drove past the Hi-Line, a roadside watering hole in Lanesville, I recognized Eino's truck parked outside. I stopped and joined him in the gloomy bar, where he was nursing a beer, or a whiskey, or possibly one of each. He bought me a Coke, and in our quiet conversation, I sensed both his melancholy and kindheartedness.

Eino never married, as far as I know, but he was related to many of Gloucester's artists through his extensive family. His sister Saima married the renowned sculptor Walker Hancock. Eino's brother Jimo, Isabel's father, married Pauline, the daughter of Paul Manship, creator of the famous gilded Art-Deco *Prometheus* at Rockefeller Center in New York. This mingling of creative artists and the Finnish community was a distinctive feature of life in Folly Cove, and for me an eye-opener. Celebrated artists could live simply, surrounded by natural beauty.

⚜

Another of Eino's brothers, Robert Natti, was married to Lee Kingman, a respected author, editor, and Folly Cove designer, and Jinnee's good friend. Early on, Jinnee introduced me to Robert and Lee at their wood-fired sauna near the Natti home at Blood Ledge Quarry. Lee, with her short, wavy, steel-gray hair, had a warm, calming presence and an intelligent, confidence-inspiring manner. Robert was a teacher and counselor at Gloucester High School and had a small home pottery studio.

They generously opened their wood-fired sauna bath to invitees. I learned that after entering the sauna and undressing, your lungs struggle to adapt to the sharp, dry heat inside and the occasional bursts of scalding steam that surge when someone ladles water onto radiant rocks. In our "first sitting" we gently thrashed our legs, arms, and backs—and anywhere else we could reach—with supple birch boughs bound in bunches to relax muscles and exfoliate skin. An interlude followed for a quick soaping or shampoo and a rinse with water poured from a wooden bucket. A cold beer and conversation in the cooler anteroom followed. Then we gathered again in the 150-degree sauna for a proper cleansing sweat.

To finish, the grand finale: naked, we sprinted and plunged into the clear cold water of the quarry, just steps away, to close our wide-open pores and wake us up.

Finns schedule the women's sauna time separately from the men's, and the fun of skinny dipping with a high-spirited, multi-generational group of women proved refreshing for body and spirit—and not nearly so awkward as I'd first imagined.

⸎

Norman von Rosenvinge, who lived in the town of Rockport, was Jinnee's Boston lawyer. He also served as the Danish consul in Massachusetts. Norman was aptly named—a man of the North, tall, formidable in physical stature, with a large head and a sharp nose. He had an opinionated, take-charge personality and was a frequent visitor at George and Jinnee's, especially for poker evenings.

In their home overlooking the sea, the hospitable von Rosenvinge family specialized in serving cocktails, grilling steak, and cranking homemade ice cream. Their spacious shingled house was filled with art books and paintings. Norman and his wife had six children: I became friends with Tycho, who had just graduated from college, and his younger brother Nik, a high-school junior. Tycho's generosity included quarry-side picnics with sandwiches washed down with

Carlsberg and sails to nearby islands. Nik invited me to join him on his morning lobster run, an unexpected and exciting prospect that broadened my perspective on Cape Ann life.

⸎

Fen Lasell, an author/illustrator of children's books, was in her early thirties. She embodied natural elegance—tall and leggy, she gathered her long, honey-blond hair in a loose bun at her neck. She wore peasant skirts and blouses. Her feet were often bare and her shoulders draped with a hand-woven shawl. I found her aura exotic and sexy. I searched Rockport for a similar wrap but, in my price range, the closest I could come was a blue-and-gray winter scarf arranged poncho-like and fastened with a safety pin.

⸎

A few houses away from Jinnee's on Washington Street lived Giovanna Calastri Lawford, an artist and author, and her husband, Geoffrey Lawford, a New York architect.

Giovanna had been a student of George's. Her slim book *The Human Frame*, with a foreword by anthropologist Margaret Mead, offers simple, accurate line drawings of the body's bones and articulations. "The structure of the body deserves as much admiration as its outward surface," Giovanna wrote in her introduction. "The farther we reach into the treasure house of our bodies, the more we discover of greatness of design and beauty of form."

Giovanna was exquisite to behold, with a calm brow and straight nose, her brown hair parted in the middle and braids circling her head like an Italian Madonna. I thought that if I ever had a daughter, I would name her Giovanna. She was Jinnee's confidante, and one day Jinnee invited me along to the Lawfords' cozy house for a coffee.

At a certain point, Jinnee confessed the pain she endured at her periodontist's office while undergoing treatments for her teeth and gums. I've not forgotten Giovanna's cheerful advice from her own experience: "Open up to the pain! Embrace it! I speak to the pain directly. I say to it: 'Is *that* the worst you can do? I can take more! Give me more!'"

At another memorable moment, the two commiserated over their husbands' numerous irritable outbursts. Including me in their intimate banter, they laughingly agreed that there must certainly be such a thing as male menopause.

<hr />

George and Jinnee kindly invited me to go along with them to various social occasions—once, a cocktail party at Starfield, sculptor Paul Manship's domain, with its modest late-nineteenth-century house perched on the edge of a quarry and an old barn studio.

In my diary, I recorded:

> It was fascinating. Again, the average age of the party-goers was sixty-five or seventy, except for a ten-year-old guest named Pearl..... The house overlooks a quarry with lily pads.... It reflected the setting sun. The house seems very old and the kitchen fascinating—and huge: old wooden icebox and big stove—low ceiling—long, narrow table in the middle of the floor. There are grape arbors and a barn studio where Manship's son John's paintings are displayed.... I walked around and looked at the sculpture in the yard. We left at 7:30.

<hr />

As I watched Jinnee and George interact with others, their two complex personalities came more sharply into focus. While George played the expansive host at larger gatherings, Jinnee formed friendships and working collaborations, making closer connections. I observed how her confident but usually understated manner encouraged and supported others, in private and public. I felt this, too, in our relationship. She may not have been emotionally effusive—there were few hugs and little explicit praise—but her matter-of-factness was grounded in tolerance and patience, up to a point.

Though at times Jinnee remarked that she wasn't feeling well, I wasn't aware until much later that she was suffering from serious health problems. In 1963, she may not yet have been fully aware of her condition. That summer, though, she seemed content to stay at home and putter about, drawing, printing some designs, reading mysteries, and, later in the day, walking out to the Point for a swim or a sunset.

Neighbors Notes

***When you paint a background you are painting all that volume of space which is the setting of your subject...the air he* breathes:** Henri, *The Art Spirit*, page 41.

***Drove to Gloucester for a dance class*:** Ina Hahn's studio at that time was on Center Street. Later in the 1960s, she and her husband converted a Rockport dairy farm into the Windhover Center for the Performing Arts. In 2001, Hahn and her dancers created a dance/theater work, *Made in Folly Cove*, a tribute to the Folly Cove Designers' lives and work.

***Fen was an author/illustrator*:** her book *Michael Grows a Wish* was published in 1962.

Eino A. Natti (1909–1975), *Yo Heave Ho*, 1953, ink on linen, linoleum block print. Collection of the Cape Ann Museum, Gloucester, MA.

Chapter Nine

Seascape

…the only education that counts is self-education.

Jinnee, George, and their friends introduced me to Cape Ann's art and the area's elemental rocks, woods, and sea. When neighbor Norman von Rosenvinge's younger son Nik invited me to go along on his morning lobster run, I was eager to venture out on the water in a small boat. I wanted to drift on the big ocean and to look on the town of Rockport, nestled below the steeple of the 1804 First Congregational Church, from a new perspective.

Early one foggy morning, I stood on T-wharf in my windbreaker and Wellingtons while Nik pulled a waterproof yellow coverall over his stained khakis and knee-high rubber boots. Whistling Dylan's "Blowin' in the Wind," he fastened the suspenders over his sweatshirt and commented on the worn places in both his trousers and boots. Since he'd been spending so much time in the boat, he said, he went through clothes pretty fast.

He grabbed a yellow slicker from the back seat of his old Ford and slammed the door. He put on the jacket and yawned. The sun wasn't yet up. The sky was gray, and it was too early to tell whether it would burn through the fog—it could last all morning.

He wrestled the bait can out of the trunk. His old pail had rotted through the bottom, but this one was a galvanized garbage can guaranteed for life. It was filled with fish scraps from the cannery over on the Gloucester docks where the Portuguese fishing boats came in. He carried the heavy load two-handed from the car to the pulley rig at the edge of the paved wharf. Even before dawn, seven or eight station wagons were parked there. They belonged to fishermen who went out at 3:30 or 4 a.m. after a couple of cups of coffee around the corner at Ellen's Restaurant.

If not for the heavy fog, the gray-shingled Yacht Club at the end of the wharf and the tall masts of Star boats on their trailers would be visible. In the quiet, I heard halyards drumming against the swaying masts of boats moored in the inner harbor, rising and falling with the swells.

In a few hours, there wouldn't be a parking place within a mile of town. They'd be selling popcorn in the Kiwanis booth down the wharf. There'd be sightseeing boats leaving every half hour and Ladies' Sailing Classes at the club. Amateur artists would set up their easels on the hot asphalt between parked cars, painting seascapes and lobster shacks.

On the wharf, Nik fastened the pulley's hook onto the handle of the bait bucket before lowering it to his boat. It was low tide, and the skiff was half stuck in the mud. Nik climbed down the ladder and pulled the boat around to float it in the shallow water before climbing in. Then, using the pulley rig, he lowered the pail, set it in the boat, unfastened the line, and hoisted the hook back up to the top. Finally, he threw the free end of the pulley rope back up onto the wharf where I was waiting.

Nik sat for a moment in the stern before he put the outboard's propeller into the water. The sun still had not risen, or, at least, it was not visible through the fog. This could be a problem. If he went out one more morning before sunup without running lights, the Coast Guard would be sure to get him—especially since he had to pass by the station at Gap Head on his way to his traps in Whale Cove.

I climbed slowly and inexpertly down the ladder, stepped into the boat, and sat quickly as Nik picked up the bailer cut from a plastic Clorox jug and started to empty out bilge water. The bait can was centered between the wooden seats in the middle of the fifteen-foot skiff. Next to me was a basket containing a limp piece of burlap sacking, a small box of wooden wedges, a brass lobster gauge, a stiff old glove, and a knife. In the bottom of the boat lay a set of battered oars and an orange life jacket.

Now the fog seemed to be clearing. Though it was still hazy, Nik cast us off and started the small motor. He handled it well—better than he drove a car. But then, at seventeen, he'd been handling boats longer than he'd been driving. I'd soon begin my junior year in college and viewed Nik with a certain amused detachment. I considered myself older and more experienced—though definitely not around boats.

Nik maneuvered out of the harbor at a speedy clip, considering the poor visibility. Offshore the air was clearer. The water was choppy and, as the boat picked up speed, the spray blew wetter. We waved to another lobsterman, a fat man in a black oilcloth apron, who had a larger boat with a winch to haul his traps and save his back.

We turned through the narrows, passing between Straitsmouth Island with its abandoned lighthouse and the rocky mainland shore, where a white cross commemorated a girl swept to sea twenty years earlier. We passed summer cottages, a stretch of sand beach, a resort hotel, the Coast Guard station tower, and the twin lighthouses on Thacher Island, then spotted Nik's family's house, still dark. A foghorn moaned. As we surveyed the familiar quiet shore, herring gulls swooped around the boat. Some of the birds were white. The speckled brown ones were under a year old, Nik explained. Uninhabited Milk Island, farther along to the south, was chalky with their droppings.

Nik slowed down, looking for his first buoy. He had painted his markers with red, white, and gray stripes. He spotted his own colors among hundreds of others, circled the boat around, and idled the motor. Leaning over the side, he caught the buoy, threw it into the boat, and began to haul in the line, hand-over-hand. It was one of his oldest traps, and the rope was limp and soggy, hung with kelp and hair-like sea moss.

Bracing one leg against the gunwale, he strained to haul up the trap itself. When it broke the surface, gushing water through the wooden slats, he hoisted it onto the edge of the skiff and peered in before he opened it. There were just four or five crabs. Impatiently, Nik threw out all but one, then cracked its shell against the gunwale and put it into the trap for bait. Frustrated by the bare fish bones left on the hook inside, he took a fresh fish head from the can and shoved the large wire hook through both eyes. He closed the trap and threw it back in.

Our small boat had drifted. Nik got his bearings and headed for Number 2, hoping for at least one good lobster. If he ever got around to making more traps—the slats and nails and line were still on his family's back porch—he said he could have fifty out by the end of summer.

"More traps, more lobsters, more money," Nik figured, though he didn't think he'd be needing the money for college. He supposed he could go if he studied hard his senior year, but after high school, he was thinking of going into the paratroopers for a while. His father said the reason Nik didn't make good grades in school was that he wasn't paid for it—but the fact was, he didn't like boarding school. He liked the guys at Gloucester High School better. And he liked being alone a lot, which was hard when you lived in a dorm. Mostly, he said, he loved the summer when he could be on his own and not think about school. I imagined he liked how his skin tightened when the sea spray evaporated and left salty spots on his face and hands, and the August sun warmed the back of his neck.

Number 2 was wrapped around another buoy. Nik untangled the lines and hauled up the trap. Two lobsters looked big enough before he measured them, but they turned out to be shorts.

"Why don't you grow up?" he muttered, no doubt echoing his father. He threw them into the water, baited the hook, and shoved Number 2 back in with a splash.

The sun had begun to burn through the fog as we sped toward Number 3. Nik idled the motor, caught the buoy, and started to haul. The rope was cold and soft between his fingers as his arms stretched and his shoulder muscles strained. Inside the trap were three shorts, one legal-sized lobster, and a huge seeder—a female laden with eggs.

He threw the shorts and the seeder into the water and picked up the prize behind its pincer claws. As I watched, he inserted wooden wedges in the hinges of the larger and smaller claw and put the keeper in the basket. Leaning over the side, he dipped the burlap in seawater, then covered the basket. Once again, he baited the hook and threw the trap back in.

He didn't mind the repetitive work; the rhythms plainly made him feel competent, efficient, and self-sufficient. He maneuvered the boat skillfully and hailed fellow lobstermen with professional nods as we passed. As the sun burned through the fog and the air warmed, Nik steered us from trap to trap at a leisurely pace. I started to feel relaxed out on the water.

Number 17 was located on the far side of Straitsmouth Island. A cool sea breeze lifted waves against the surrounding boulders. The buoy appeared farther in among the rocks than Nik had remembered. The tide had turned; the approach was tricky.

"Keep an eye peeled," he warned me—and himself.

He took it slow and kept a steady gaze on his objective. The buoy was easy to recover, but the trap was difficult since it was weighted with bricks, and the boat kept edging closer to the island. After he lunged for the trap and heaved it into the boat, he grabbed an oar. He tried to push off from the rocks, but the breeze had shifted, and the incoming tide was against him. It was all he could do to keep an oar's length away. He was afraid the propeller would hit a stone or get stuck in the sand. He stopped and pulled up the prop. Gulls shrieked overhead, and I began to feel anxious.

Nik scanned the water for other boats, silently hoping no one was watching. He stood up and let the boat drift a little closer toward the rocks so he could place the blade of the oar squarely against a hard surface. He squinted, flexed his knees and elbows, and then shoved as hard as he could. Once out of dangerously shallow water, Nik started the motor and carefully turned the boat. Finally, when we were far enough away, he slid the still unopened trap and buoy over the side, relieved just to escape.

"Brother," he said. "Not too cool a move, getting so close."

It seemed warmer. Nik took his jacket off over his head, smoothed his hair. He leaned over to check on his catch in the burlap-covered basket.

"Only five lobsters from seventeen traps. And just thirteen to go. Five lobsters. Oh, well."

He rechecked the bait can. About half full. So far, he was judging it about right.

"Well, hell," he said, "there are still thirteen more traps. And tomorrow is another day. And I really don't need the money—I have enough to get by on."

He could take care of himself.

Nik yanked in the next buoy. I saw him become conscious of his own strength as he hauled in the rope line and heaved the trap into the boat. He baited the hook in a single elegant gesture, and I suspected he might be picturing the way he looked. He pitched the trap into the water and followed it with the buoy in a perfect arc.

Neither of us had a watch, but judging by the sun, we figured it must be about nine o'clock. The next buoy was waiting directly offshore from the venerable Sea View Inn, where several guests were eating breakfast on the stately wraparound porch. Some of them had binoculars, and others were waving to him. Nik glanced at them before scooping up the buoy with its dripping green line. His hands hurt from rope burn, but the glove had fallen to the bottom of the boat, soaked and useless.

Nik bent his head and opened the trap. More crabs and another big seeder.

"The seeders are always the best ones," he said, annoyed, as he baited the hook again. He picked up the large lobster loaded with eggs and faced the inn—might as well give the crowd a thrill. He held the blue-green lobster aloft for a long moment for the guests to admire. It was large and speckled, claws and feelers flapping wildly. The visitors waved approval. Then he casually tossed it into the water, followed shortly by the baited trap and buoy. He smiled at me, gunned the motor, and didn't look back.

We were almost to the end of the run now, back in the Outer Harbor. It was Saturday—Race Day. The gray-shingled Yacht Club looked busy. People were lowering the Star-class sailboats into the water, and a crowd was waiting on the wharf for the tour boat. Little boys in sailboats reminded Nik of past summers.

He repeated the process of hauling, baiting, and releasing the remaining dozen traps. He didn't miss one—but he really had to get those new traps made the next week. Not too much of summer left. It was slipping away.

I leaned to trail my hand over the stern, watching the water foam white around the small propeller and feeling its cool froth. Sunshine reflected on every ripple, a million dancing stars.

The skiff circled and headed for the Inner Harbor entrance, red light to the right, then slowed to no-wake speed, avoiding two outbound Stars.

"Hey, Nik, good catch?" called Dave and Trina from their boat. They were rigging sails for the race.

"Okay. About nine."

Tourists on the dock took snapshots as Nik headed the boat smoothly up to the wharf. After tying up at the ladder, he scrambled up, took off his coverall and jacket, and left them on the wharf. Then I climbed up, and Nik used the pulley for the empty bait can and again for the basket of lobsters. Collecting all our stuff, we walked back to the car and threw our sweatshirts into the backseat, locking the gear and the bait can in the trunk.

Nik picked up the basket, and we headed down to Eddie Donovan's lobster pound to sell the catch. Eddie would pay him cash on the barrelhead. The take wouldn't be bad this week—lots of people wanting lobsters and not many guys catching any. He planned to go over to Ellen's and get some breakfast and blueberry pie and then down to Quinlan's for another look at the red shirt he'd been eyeing. That might just wipe out today's earnings, but with a little luck, he'd make twice that when he'd set twenty more traps.

I smiled to see young tourists in sundresses turn to watch as we threaded our way down Bearskin Neck with the basket of live lobsters. I admired Nik's playful energy.

"A little more local color." He laughed, satisfied with his morning's work and pleased with the approving glances from his audience.

Seascape Notes

The only education that counts is self-education: Henri, *The Art Spirit*, page 211.

Virginia Lee Demetrios (1909–1968), *Gossips*, undated, ink on
linen, linoleum block print. Collection of the Cape Ann Museum,
Gloucester, MA. Gift of Betty Hills, 1994 (1994.1.1).

Chapter Ten

Late Summer

To be honest is to be just, and to be just is to realize the relative value of things.

I N August, Jinnee explained to my grandparents that

> June has fitted in to the Demetrios ménage without effort. It has been a pleasure to have her with us.... As I told you on the telephone, I advised her to spend less time on her job at the bookstore.... The hours are too long and I think it is more important that she learns drawing from George.... [And] I can give her a beginning course in design.

This design course met less often than I would have liked, but on Saturdays, I helped out with inventory and sales at the busy Folly Cove Designers Barn retail showroom up Route 127, just before the Rockport line.

During my stay, I seemed to become something of a project for Jinnee and George. They were modeling an attitude toward living as well as making art. Along with drawing instruction, design lessons, and dinner conversation over wine, they encouraged me with novels, philosophy, poetry, and art books.

My bedroom bookcase had opened new worlds: Rilke's *Letters to a Young Poet* ("Let life happen to you. Believe me, life is in the right, always."); pioneering classical scholar Edith Hamilton's *The Greek Way*; Mary Renault's myth about a myth, *The King Must Die*; John Updike's *Pigeon Feathers*; and the rich catalog of paintings and nineteenth-century culture from the Isabella Stewart Gardner Museum.

Jinnee and George invited me into larger conversations, and though I was mostly silent with adult visitors, they paid attention when I did venture to contribute. With Jinnee and George, I felt at home—accepted and supported.

Yet I was truly thankful for a few acquaintances my own age. Three of them, all boys, kept life busy with picnics, dances, concerts, museum visits, and sailing. Now, when I read over my summer journal, the level of activity seems remarkably hectic. What an assortment of people! How much energy I had! How little transition time I required, and how late I could stay up and still function the next day! We made plans, then changed or canceled them, and recalibrated. New schemes would be cooked up at the last minute, and we all went with the flow. I learned to be more spontaneous than I had ever been, more confident in my ability "to let life happen," testing limits yet remaining vigilant.

I was imagining a more observant, social, spur-of-the-moment, even risk-taking self—in art-making and in everyday life. But I wasn't aware that my behavior might ring alarm bells. I now think that for Jinnee, tracking a nineteen-year-old niece in 1963 and making sure she was safe was probably trickier than watching over her two sons in the '40s and '50s. Even though I considered myself level-headed, Jinnee and George may have been wary of potential danger on their watch. The most perilous, scandalous though unspoken predicament of all would have been an unwanted pregnancy. Jinnee and George were responsible for me and answerable to my parents and grandparents.

So, I sensed that while they seemed to be liberating me from my accustomed norms, they also expected me to remain neat, helpful, modest, reliable, and above reproach, especially with boys. And in fact, my superego required it, too.

≪≪≪≫

Jinnee shared her birthday, August 30, with her son Mike, whom she missed sorely: he was working in Europe that summer. George had planned a small birthday celebration. Unlike the old days, when birthday parties might draw eighty-five guests for an outdoor barbecue with singing and dancing, this one would include only a few close friends.

Virginia Lee Burton Demetrios and George Demetrios, ca.
1960s. Photograph by William E. Smith. Image courtesy of the
Cape Ann Museum Library & Archives, Gloucester, MA.

Before the gathering that Friday evening, they were expecting an
interviewer from the *Gloucester Daily Times* who would feature George
for the paper's weekly profile. "Sculptor Lover of Life" appeared
a week or so later, alongside a picture of Jinnee and George in the
living room, George holding his bust of Mike as a smiling child. His
sculpture of Aris, a little older and more introspective, gazed down
from the shelf above them. The photo must have been snapped from
over near the front staircase, where his striking bronze bust of Jinnee,
"Virginia Lee," crowned the newel post.

Since I wasn't expected to be present for the interview or to join
them later for their get-together with friends, I wished Jinnee a happy
birthday with a quick kiss and left for the evening. One of the boys
Mrs. Dangerfield had warned me about had invited me to a party
that night at his family's summer rental in East Gloucester. He'd

become a friend, someone who'd visited the Boston MFA with me to see drawings.

The house was an unusual old building with an interior balcony overlooking a spacious, high-ceilinged living room. I remember liking its theatrical Shakespearean atmosphere. Though I don't recall party snacks or dinner, there was plenty of white wine.

I had seldom taken a drink, even beer, before arriving at college. The requisite freshman-weekend whiskey sours and rum Cokes had left me wary of mixed drinks. But I had become quite fond of white wine. Today, I don't remember anything about the party or who was there. Afterward, I was too embarrassed even to write about it in my diary. I do remember an exciting group exodus to a beach, in several cars. Then, lying on the sand next to my date. I liked him well enough, and though at a certain point I imagined throwing caution to the wind (for once!), I fell asleep instead. We woke up near dawn, exhausted, parched, rumpled, and bleary. My hair was caked with sand.

⋘⋙

About 4:30 a.m., as the sky was glowing pink, we drove back to Folly Cove. We turned in to the long drive and drove slowly toward the house, car windows open for fresh air and headlights switched off. Ahead, Jinnee was clearly visible at the kitchen door, leaning over the porch railing as we approached. The overhead light illuminated her blue robe. My date hung his head and mumbled as he gripped the steering wheel. I opened the car door slowly, got out, and shut the door. The car backed up to turn, then drove away.

Jinnee was furious. She had been worried sick. The police were searching for us. Why hadn't I thought to call? Would I have done such a thing at home?

The truth was, yes. At home, no news was good news. Neither my mother nor my father was a hands-on parent: they often left us three daughters to our own devices, trusting and content as long as we didn't disturb life's surface. But now, I had ruined Jinnee's birthday. I was embarrassed and humiliated, and so sorry.

Jinnee spun around and opened the kitchen door. Despairingly, I followed her. Of course, why wouldn't she jump to the conclusion that I had been ravished? And why wouldn't she be upset, imagining my possible ruin? I stammered my apologies. Not knowing what more to say, or how to make amends, I trailed her slowly up the stairs and collapsed on my bed.

I was due at the Designers Barn at 8:30 that Saturday morning. I awoke just in time, dressed quickly, and ran to the barn, hair still encrusted with sand. A group of mutely disapproving Designers met me there. I worked silently, head down, folding and arranging tablecloths, runners, placemats, and aprons.

As guilty as I felt, and as repentant, I admired Jinnee's integrity and forthrightness. She cared. She personified the kind of authenticity I'd noticed on my first day among the guests at the June picnic. I vowed to become more honest myself, not only with Jinnee and other adults but also with the boys I dated and sailed and picnicked with. I longed for more open and truthful communication, in contrast to Mrs. Dangerfield's lack of candor and my parents' silences.

Aris once described his mother to an interviewer as "emotionally absolutely pure…whatever she registered—joy or whatever it was.… [And,] if she didn't like something, God, it was *whammo*, it came out. She was just so wonderfully honest."

I had fallen short of Jinnee's expectations and contributed to her unhappy birthday. Still, after this *whammo* she did not appear to bear me ill will. She seemed to recognize that staying out till dawn had been thoughtless but not malicious. Even now, as I squirm to remember this episode, I wonder whether Jinnee might have recalled youthful follies of her own.

Late Summer Notes

To be honest is to be just, and to be just is to realize the relative value of things: Henri, *The Art Spirit*, page 93.

Jinnee explained to my grandparents: letter from VLB to Selma and Harold, August 2, 1963.

Aris once described his mother: Cape Ann Museum (CAM) Folly Cove Designers Archive Collection A78, box #5, interviews by Professor Penny Martin: Interview with Aris Demetrios, San Francisco, CA, June 25, 1993.

Virginia Lee Demetrios (1909–1968), *Early Bird*, 1965, ink on linen, linoleum block print. Collection of the Cape Ann Museum, Gloucester, MA.

CHAPTER ELEVEN

Early Spring 1964

*The most vital things in the look of a face or of a landscape endure for only
a moment. Work should be done from memory…of that vital moment.*

THE LAST GREEN-GOLD DAYS OF MY SUMMER OF 1963 WERE A FLURRY
of farewell visits, meals, boat trips, gifts, and ice cream. Friends
and cousins, aunts and uncles arrived to stay with us in the house.
We made lobster dinners with steamed clams and roast lamb with
eggplant and egg and lemon sauce.

In late August, we read about the successful March on Washington
and watched Reverend Martin Luther King's stirring "I Have a
Dream" speech. Later in September, I was back at college. The
Ebenezer Baptist Church in Birmingham, Alabama, was bombed.
In November, President John F. Kennedy was assassinated in Dallas,
and Lyndon Johnson became president. The country was in turmoil,
and the '60s became "The Sixties."

That fall semester, I returned to Cape Ann once for a respite and
visited again for a weekend the following March. The day before I
arrived, a nor'easter had roiled the slate-gray sea, and the weather
was still cold and misty. I pulled up my hood as I walked to the big
boulders standing guard above Rockport's Back Beach. The wind
lifted the waves high, spraying surf onto granite rocks. Gulls on shore
jumped the breakers that rolled in and lapped the pebbly beach. I
moved closer to study the birds' hunting and pecking but saw only
small stones worn smooth by past storms.

The sand was wet and hard and the light breeze smelled faintly
salty. Behind me, in the soft, dim drizzle, the street was empty. The
hanging signs at the inns and shops along the way had been taken
down. The foghorns lowed softly. It was 4:30 in the afternoon, and

the sky was turning royal blue. I watched for a while longer, remembering the summer's warmth. Seabirds bobbed in the surf where bathers had frolicked in the August sun.

I headed back to the car, remembering that here we rode bikes, and over there, we bought ice cream cones. With bare feet, I had walked gingerly in the shadows of store awnings on this stretch of sidewalk when it was scorching hot. Once, in the early morning before work, I'd played alone on the swing set behind the school.

After work, on bright, humid summer days, there'd been plenty of time to climb down the hot granite boulders for a dip in the ocean—so cold your skin tingled and felt smooth and cool after you got out and sat on the flat rocks to warm up.

<hr>

Toward noon the next day, from upstairs, I heard Aili shooing Zaidee off the warming ledge on the big black stove. I imagined her down in the kitchen making lunch, carefully testing a spoonful of simmering soup. I went down to join her.

Aili Runsala was round and fair, with rosy Finnish cheeks and a merry, puckish look, her thin brown hair caught on the top of her head in a washerwoman's knot. Her arms were short but her movements graceful as she stirred the steaming, fragrant fish chowder. Her feet assumed their naturally forty-five degree, turned-out position: endearingly, she resembled a pudgy ballerina in white anklets and Keds.

Then, a loud voice from the doorway: "Hi, hi, Aili. Jinnee up?"

Aili, startled, still holding the wooden spoon: "Oh! Well, no. I don't know. She's up in her room, I think, sir."

George hung his sweater over the back of the kitchen chair. "Jinnee!" he called. "You up? Feeling better?" He left the room and tramped upstairs. "Jinnee! You feeling better?" We listened as he walked into her bedroom above. I knew she was sitting in bed, propped up with pillows, her long hair loose, holding a detective novel. As he entered, she would have taken off the reading glasses that hung on a gold chain around her neck and let them fall to her chest. From the kitchen I could hear their voices.

"Hi, George."

"Are you coming down for lunch? Want a little drink? A little whiskey for the cold?"

"You know, I'm just reading one of those new mysteries Mike brought me last fall. It's a good thing he did. I've been through all my old ones twice, and then it's no fun."

"Bah, what a woman. Will you come downstairs for lunch, or do you want us to bring you a tray?"

"I'm not hungry, George. But I am feeling a little better."

"Oh, you're feeling better, all right. I can tell. Oh yes, you're feeling better because you're starting to talk back again. I was wondering when you'd begin showing a little life. All right, come down and keep us company if you're feeling so fine. And have a little whiskey. It's good for you."

"Aili!" he shouted as he headed back down the steep stairs, "let's go. I'm hungry. I've been working in the garden all morning. That's hard work, you know."

Aili and I had set four places and put bread and butter, plates, and soup bowls on the square wooden table. She ladled the steaming broth into the bowls.

"Good morning, Aili and June," Jinnee said, walking into the kitchen. We sat down as George washed his hands in the sink.

"Oh!" Aili said in her mildly startled way. "Feeling better, Mrs. Demetrios?"

"Well, yes, a little better," Jinnee said.

"Now, let's eat," George said to her. "See, I've washed my hands for you, and I got the nails clean." He spread out his fingers and turned his hands over as proof.

"Working in the garden is hard work, you know. But we'll have the first tomatoes early this year, you'll see. Oh, yes, it's hard work, all right. Keeps me from spending time getting those pictures ready to send to the galleries. But I'm almost done with that, too. Mr. Brown did some fine work on those pictures. It's hard to photograph sculpture, you know. The light makes the difference. The light and the angles. It's hard not to distort them, you know. I was just cutting them down to put them into the albums yesterday.

"I have most of the latest work there, but I think I'll enter that old one—the cast is still up in the studio. The *Early Spring in Massachusetts*, you know, with the four men leaning to look at the girl whose skirt is blowing in the wind. Well, I know it's a little different from the *Pan*, but you can't be serious all the time, you know.

"A little chowder, Jinnee? Some cheese? *Du pain?* Well, you know you're going to have to eat more."

"Good chowder, George," Jinnee said.

"M-mm-mm," Aili said, her head bent to her spoon, her eyes looking up at us from the bowl.

"That's the last of what was in the freezer from last summer. Isn't it almost time for you and Papa to go down to the Point and start fishing again?" Jinnee said.

"Well, yes, yes, of course, Jinnee, but I haven't had a chance to *talk* to him."

"Why don't you call him after lunch?" Jinnee said.

"I'll have to call Papa," George said. "I miss Papa and Mary. Are you well enough so I can ask them for dinner and a little poker this Friday? We haven't seen them for a long time, you know. That Papa—wonderful man. You know Papa Greer, Aili?"

"Yes, sir. I met Mr. Greer one time. Last winter, I think it was."

"Well, Jinnee, are you well enough to have our old friends come on Friday? Last week you were too sick, remember. Before that, it must have been Mary's mother again. What a woman she is. She won't even let Papa have a cigarette in his own house because she hates smoke. She's wrecked Mary's chance to become an artist because she has to take care of her all the time. Oh, Mary could have become a great artist. What a wonderful, sensitive person."

"And Papa too, George," Jinnee said.

"Yes, and, of course, Papa hasn't been able to do the research for his book because of that mother. But they can't get rid of her, I suppose. And *he* wants whatever Mary wants. It's a shame, those two. Such creative people and stuck in the middle of such a family. And Mary, instead of painting as she should be doing, and Papa, instead of writing, they're all caught up in this social work thing. They want to help in the slums of Gloucester. They think they are going to clean up human beings. What a waste! Two such wonderful people, and they can't live their own lives and use their own talents. They can't even straighten out their own family, and they want to help the poor of Gloucester lead better lives. Well, it just can't be done. And if Papa and Mary were really interested in helping humanity, they'd develop themselves instead of trying to give baths to the slums of Gloucester."

I was holding my breath. I exhaled.

George paused, then continued. "Papa is my oldest and dearest friend, Jinnee, but I have to watch him waste his life. Well. We'll have them to dinner on Friday, then. Okay. I get mad every time I think about it, you know. Maybe when they come here, they can forget some of this mess and relax. Papa can smoke all the cigarettes he wants in my house, you know."

George threw down his napkin. "I'm going to call *right now*."

He stood and went to the telephone on the hall table by the back stairs.

"Jinnee! What's the number?"

"It's in the book there, George."

"Oh, yes, the book. Goddammit. Where *is* it?"

Finally, he dialed, and we heard him shouting into the phone, as he always did.

He was booming, "Papa, *mon vieux*…"

"He gets so excited lately," Jinnee said softly. "He's been working too hard on that exhibit he wants in New York. I don't know if he'll ever get it. They don't like his kind of sculpture there. All they want in the galleries is welded pig-iron or pictures of Campbell's soup cans. He's upset, and he's working too hard."

"He was out in the garden all morning," Aili said quietly.

Jinnee sat staring out the window. She hadn't finished her chowder. The ewes and the lambs were grazing peacefully. Donny

had cornered Sam the Ram and removed him. The trees were beginning to leaf, and now you couldn't see down the driveway any farther
than the mailbox. Washington Street was already hidden. The
swallows were swooping again, along with an occasional circling gull.
The garden was showing even rows of neatly weeded green sprouts
in the dark, rich, well-watered earth.

"Maybe he shouldn't work so hard in that garden of his," Jinnee
said.

"Oh, Mrs. Demetrios, he couldn't stop doing that!" Aili said,
taking some chocolate chip cookies from the half-filled jar. Aili
baked cookies once a week and, although neither Jinnee nor George
ate desserts, and Mike had been away for six years, the cookie jar
emptied rapidly.

"Oh, I know. But Aili, he's almost seventy now. And working is
still the only way he can relax."

"Except for watching television," Aili said, hunching her shoulders and giggling silently. Her round face, small nose, crinkly eyes,
and topknot made her look like a mischievous imp. Sometimes
George asked her to pose for the summer portrait classes. This she
took in stride, and she was always anxious to see what people had
drawn. She praised their drawings, though privately, she thought
they never captured her true expression.

"Yes, the television," Jinnee said dryly. I smiled.

George came back after his call.

"All right, it's all right, Jinnee. They're coming. Papa and Mary
are coming Friday, all right. They said to tell you hello. Well. I'm
glad that's settled. It'll be good to see them. Your *soup*, Jinnee. For
God's sake. I thought you were feeling *better*. You have to eat well. Look
at *me*. Fresh vegetables from my garden, good meat I get, good *vino*,
Aili's brown bread, a little whiskey now and then. Well, I stay healthy.
Plenty of time left before I croak, you know."

Aili drew a sharp breath and coughed, choking on a crumb.

"Well, now Aili, we're all going to go sometime, you know. But
you have to eat, Jinnee. You can't starve yourself, you know. It's true,
you don't *need* as much energy as I do—I have to work in the garden,

get the exhibit ready, write letters, teach classes—you just go out to that barn and put on a record and read those damn mystery stories and get the royalty checks."

"The mysteries are good, George. And besides, I do work. I will work when I get better. I'm sick, you know. *You* don't have bronchitis."

"There, I knew that would get her. Let's have a little spirit around here."

Jinnee lit a cigarette.

"And don't smoke that junk. Old twigs in those things. Have one of these if you're going to smoke." He reached in his shirt pocket for a small cigar.

"No *thank* you," Jinnee said.

"Bah. Sometimes I wonder about this woman's taste. She has no sense of adventure. I ask her, '*Do* you want to go to Europe and stay a little longer in Italy and Greece this time?' and she says, 'No, I want to stay here and go out to the Point and relax this summer.' I say, 'How about a party to celebrate your birthday?' and she says, 'No, the kids won't be here and we are too old to dance ourselves. It wouldn't be any fun.'"

"And don't forget how old I am!" Jinnee added.

"You know how old she is?" George asked Aili and me.

"Yes, sir. Our birthdays are exactly the same," Aili said.

"Ah," George said. "Two fifty-four-year-old babies. And look at me. I'm a hundred years old, you know, and I have more energy than both of you."

Aili giggled.

"George," Jinnee said, "are you going to teach so many classes again this summer?"

"Ah. Now you want to make *me* an invalid, too. Oh, I know there are too many classes, all right. I'm not Superman, you know. But these people keep writing me, and they want the lessons. And good people this year, Jinnee. Oh, baby, are we going to have a class. But I won't let Richard and Mildred come back. They've learned all they can from me. Time for them to start doing their own work, you know. We'll see what they can do. If only we can convince Mary to come this summer. Maybe we can get her away from that mother of hers for a little while."

"That's a good idea, George. But I think you ought to cut down on the *number* of classes."

"All right, all right, I'll see what I can do."

"You say that every spring. And every summer, you have more and more people."

"Well, somebody's got to teach them, dammit. They want to learn. And how else am I to live and make some money? And I've got a new model. Better than that redhead Louise, you know. This one works in Boston in the winter. And we'll have to have Aili, you know. Will you come, Aili? Eh?"

"For the face part, sir."

"Well, all right. If that's what you want." He winked at Jinnee. "She's a little old for nudes, don't you think?"

Aili blushed intensely and Jinnee exploded.

"*George!*"

"Ah. Her highness has spoken. Bah. The trouble with this house is two fifty-four-year-old children without a sense of humor. All right, Jinnee. Thanks for the lunch, Aili. You'll have tomatoes soon. I'm going to go take a nap. I'm a busy man this afternoon. See you later." He got up from the table and flicked cigar ash into the ashtray. "Well, what are you all so quiet about?" he asked us. "I'm going to go lie down. I can't work without some rest, you know. I'm not as young as I used to be."

I cleared the table as he strode out and started up the stairs. Jinnee whispered something to Aili, who giggled again.

"All right, Jinnee," George called out. "I can't hear you, but say what you want. I'm going to rest. Lot of things to be done around here later."

I put the dishes in the sink.

Jinnee was looking out the window toward the backyard at the spring-green apple tree and the back path winding up to George's studio. She sighed.

I imagined she was thinking that there *were* a lot of things to be done around here. The garden, dinner on Friday with Papa and

Mary, the exhibit, and before you could turn around, summer again, and his back-breaking schedule of summer classes.

I ran the water in the sink. Aili took the table scraps out to the sheep. Still seated at the table, Jinnee wondered aloud whether George's students realized how much of himself he put into teaching. She wondered if they ever really learned anything.

As I washed and rinsed the dishes, she poured a cup of coffee and lit another Pall Mall. The house was quiet.

Early Spring 1964 Notes

The most vital things in the look of a face or of a landscape endure for only a moment. Work should be done from memory...of that vital moment: Henri, *The Art Spirit*, page 31.

I miss Papa and Mary: Donald Malcolm (Papa) Greer and Mary Greer were George's longtime friends who lived in Gloucester. Mary, a painter, became deeply involved in local politics. Her husband sometimes referred to her as "the boss of Ward Six." Donald Greer was a scholar of the French Revolution, a Guggenheim Fellow, and a professor at MIT. During World War II he worked in Washington, D.C. with the Office of Strategic Services.

Virginia Lee Demetrios (1909–1968), *Swing Tree II*, undated, ink on linen, linoleum block print. Collection of the Cape Ann Museum, Gloucester, MA.

CHAPTER TWELVE

Life Stories

Your only salvation is in finding yourself…and you will never find yourself until you quit preconceiving what you will be when you have found yourself.

LIKE HER BOOKS' PLUCKY PROTAGONISTS, JINNEE CONFRONTED situations as they arose and tackled them with courage. Aris maintained that she "always came to terms with herself. She was an absolute realist. This is where the cards are dealt and I'm going to make the most of them, and I'm going to do it goddamned well."

Jinnee's health was seldom a topic of conversation during my visits, though I knew she was consulting Boston dentists for "teeth trouble." She never shared a diagnosis beyond bronchitis. She pressed ahead with determination and didn't waste time worrying.

Jinnee's family supported and reassured her. She was devoted to her sons and their families, her siblings, her half-brother Harold, and, after the death of Carl Cherry in the late 1940s, her mother. Jeanne D'Orge died in May 1964 at age 84. That summer, Jinnee traveled to Japan, where she'd been invited to give talks and workshops about her children's books. On the way home to the United States, she stopped in California for a celebration of her mother's life. Family and friends scattered Jeanne D'Orge's ashes, as she had wished, at nearby Point Lobos, her place of mystical inspiration and communion.

⁓

My grandparents, Harold and Selma, usually returned each summer to Boston, where they were married, to commemorate their anniversary, celebrate Harold's birthday, and visit Jinnee and George. But that year, 1964, Harold was coping with worsening symptoms of Parkinson's disease, and they were unable to make the trip.

Jinnee was disappointed: "Can't tell you how sorry we are that you cannot be here this year. You are both such wonderful people and we treasure the memory of your previous visits."

She concluded another note with a reference to Harold's congratulatory letter, framed and hanging on the barn studio wall: "Harold, every so often, I read that beautiful letter you sent about my last book and it makes me feel better."

In early September, Jinnee thanked them for their telephone greeting on her fifty-fifth birthday: "Your call was one of the nicest things that happened on my birthday."

When Harold passed away in late October, Jinnee sent condolences:

Dear Selma,

There is little one can say or do for you at this time—except that we are thinking of you and wanting to do whatever we can to help you.

You have been fortunate in having a little over fifty golden years of a full life with Harold. More than most people have. Always I think of you two as the perfect pair of human beings and an example of what we could be if we tried.

Selma, a special "thank you" to you for your letter to me when I was so sick. To think that you found the time and thought to write to me when you had much more important things on your mind—I was sorry not to be at the Memorial Service which my brother and sister said was very beautiful.

Ever gratefully yours, from your loving "half-sister in-law,"
Jinneeeeeeee

I traveled from college to my grandfather's memorial service in Washington, D.C., where he and my grandmother had lived for more than twenty years while he served as a senator and then as a Supreme Court justice.

During my senior year, I was dancing, writing, and finishing four years as an English major with a minor in French. My grandmother joined the family in Connecticut for my graduation in June 1965 and then traveled on to visit Jinnee at Folly Cove.

After graduation and a summer office job in stifling New York City, I left for a year of graduate study in France in September 1965, a move that turned out to be indispensable vocational training. During the succeeding five years, I found work teaching French at the primary, secondary, and college levels. While I was in France, Jinnee sent her annual hand-printed Christmas card, adding a short note: "I am sure you are having a wonderful time in Paris—when you come home you must visit us, and you and George can speak French together."

Back home the next year, I taught French in the Cleveland public schools and took graduate courses at Case-Western Reserve University. And I became engaged. After our wedding in June 1967, David and I moved to New Haven, Connecticut, where he was completing coursework in Yale's PhD program in economics. In late summer, we drove to Folly Cove, where I introduced David to Jinnee and George, and they introduced us to the new lambs at the pasture fence. As usual, they welcomed us warmly. Though Jinnee looked thinner than I remembered, I didn't suspect that it would be our final visit with her.

In the fall, I again taught French, and then, as riots set our New Haven neighborhood ablaze in the summer of 1968, David and I left the United States for a two-year teaching and research stint in East Africa. My Folly Cove tablecloths and placemats traveled with us. We washed them with our clothes in our bathtub and hung them to dry in the equatorial sunshine. But just a month or two after we arrived in Uganda, my grandmother wrote with the shocking news that Jinnee had passed away on October 15 from complications of lung cancer. I was deeply saddened to have been unaware and so far away.

Writing to Selma, who could not attend, Jinnee's sister Christine described the family memorial at Folly Point:

> It is dusk at the edge of the sea on Jinnee's own special piece of the New England coastline.... Down by the water one son appears silhouetted against the distance.... We listen.... The words are our mother's and Jinnee's own...read by her younger son. Below, her first born makes a poignant gesture, casting [her ashes] out into the unknown...

Learning more details of Jinnee's life has helped me appreciate the privilege I enjoyed when she embraced me as a family member. I deeply regret not having known Jinnee with more mature understanding than I possessed as a college girl. I might have realized more clearly her extraordinary blend of originality, skill, tenacity, confidence, and, sometimes, self-doubt. I might have been able to learn more about our family history, Jinnee's experiences as a mother and grandmother, and her marriage with George.

Most often, thinking back, I remember Jinnee's muscular, workman-like hands and her large opal ring. How she cocked her head when listening. Her gracefully absent-minded placement of a Pall Mall in her short black cigarette holder. Her strong, sturdy legs. The deft way she wielded a pencil. Her sweeping signature.

※

Jinnee loved dancing and, from a young age, dancing was my discipline and delight, too. At seven, I began ballet classes with Serge Nadejdin, an aging Russian ballet master. Throughout childhood and youth, I studied dance and choreography and later performed with the Connecticut College modern dance group. After college, wherever I found myself in the world, I continued dancing in many forms—ballet, modern, folk, African.

In 1970, somewhat by chance, we landed in Brunswick, Maine, at Bowdoin College, the alma mater of Harold's and Jinnee's father, Alfred Edgar Burton. Harold, too, had attended the school. While

David began teaching there, I taught French and English for a year at the local high school. And then, truly by chance, Bowdoin (a male bastion since 1794) admitted women for the first time in fall 1971.

Just a few months before Title IX was enacted, banning gender discrimination in educational institutions receiving federal funds, the Bowdoin administration sought activities suitable for the incoming "girls." The dean offered me an adjunct position teaching modern dance. I eagerly accepted. Gradually, my colleagues and I shaped a dance curriculum for men and women that evolved into the college's academic department of theater and dance. As a tenured professor and department chair for decades, I, with my colleagues, developed a cohesive liberal arts dance program, with studio courses in modern dance, culturally diverse techniques, and choreography, along with seminars in dance history and criticism. This unforeseen opportunity allowed me to teach, choreograph, perform, and write about movement in its many forms.

As a model and guide, Jinnee set standards for me as I faced challenges later in my life. Jinnee's methods for teaching design inspired me to devise equivalent approaches to teaching dance improvisation and composition. Her inclusive vision, and George's, with emphasis on individual investigations and collective support, meshed with the aesthetics that drove a revolution in contemporary American dance in the late1950s, '60s, and '70s. Performance could become less remote, more like life—unpredictable and full of possibilities.

The Folly Cove Designers' design process in two dimensions, which encouraged play with contrasting sizes, tones, and patterns, suggested parallels for three-dimensional choreography, juxtaposing spatial relationships, timing, and dynamics. The creative process of imagining, organizing, refining, and completing a dance matches the sequence pictured on Jinnee's Folly Cove Designers "diploma," awarded to successful designers.

Both Jinnee's and George's teaching methods invited structured exploration and reinforced my conviction that every student, with encouragement, is capable of producing original work. Students

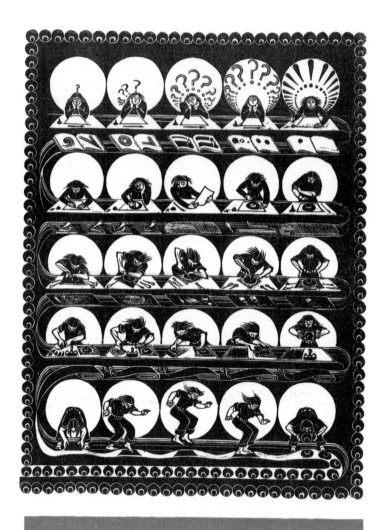

Virginia Lee Demetrios (1909–1968), *Folly Cove Designer
Diploma*, undated, ink on linen, linoleum block print.
Collection of the Cape Ann Museum, Gloucester, MA.

created dances, often within suggested frameworks. By experimenting, they perfected the technical skills needed to achieve their ambitions, beyond what they practiced in dance technique classes. At Bowdoin, we emphasized the learning process. Dance composition courses attracted and connected student artists in media such as music, film, and photography, who, like the Folly Cove Designers, formed a cross-disciplinary collaborative community. Their "serious play" produced dances rather than designs.

In 1973, after a second stint in East Africa, David and I returned to teach at Bowdoin and were again close enough to Folly Cove to pay George a visit. He greeted us among the recently installed sculptures that domesticated the backyard landscape. We admired his jubilant new piece *Jinnee Goes to Heaven*, placed on the patio where we'd enjoyed so many pleasant meals. And we strolled out to Jinnee's cottage on the Point, high above Folly Cove.

George Demetrios (1896–1974), *Jinnee Goes to Heaven*, 1970s.
Photograph from collection of the author.

George died in Gloucester on December 4, 1974. We drove from Maine with our four-month-old son Ben for the reception that overflowed the house and barn after George's memorial service in the Annisquam Village Church. We joined George's friends and neighbors, former students, and well-wishers in toasts to the legendary host.

The Cape Ann Historical Association honored George's work with a 1986 retrospective exhibit accompanied by an extensive catalog. A booklet of informal photos and testimonials by former students affirmed that George's dynamic spirit lived on:

"He was that rare being—a truly great art teacher—articulate, enthusiastic, original. But what I always felt set him above others was his great generosity to his followers."

"...he taught perception, awareness, joy."

"He was a marvelous teacher whether it was drawing and sculpture, or poker."

My favorite homage captured his charismatic, contradictory nature: "But for those of us who knew him, coughing over his ubiquitous cigars, directing and building a small world of order and beauty and encouraging striving would-be artists, he was a lovable and demanding, shrewd and forgiving, figure who always seemed larger than life."

George's exhortations still echo in my own thoughts: "See the whole thing! See the relative values! Everything fits together!"

≪≪≪⌐

When David and I visited Cape Ann in 2002, new owners were renovating Jinnee and George's small house. A dumpster stood in the driveway, the sheep pasture was full of saplings, and the old apple tree behind the house had disappeared. Across Route 127, Jinnee's Folly Point retreat had been sold, but the now dilapidated writing cottage still perched there, slated for demolition. The lane and overgrown footpath out to the Point had been transformed into a paved road, colonized by vacation homes and manicured estates with underground sprinkler systems.

By the fall of 2013, my cousin Ross (Sandy) Burton had salvaged and relocated Jinnee's writing cottage. He became the prime mover in efforts to bring the decrepit cabin back to life on a site next to the Lanesville Community Center. In Jinnee's honor, he and the project's many local sponsors and volunteers restored the tiny cottage, echoing the survival story of *The Little House*. They reimagined it as a home for children's art activities and writing programs, storybook readings, and workshops. Dedicated community members and other supporters accomplished a remarkable feat, retaining much of the original structure while rehabilitating, rebuilding, and replacing as necessary.

The cottage renovation was completed in fall 2018, and on a bright and breezy October day, the Cape Ann community celebrated the official opening of the VLB Writing Cottage. It was a fitting tribute to Jinnee's conviction that art fosters both individual growth and community vitality. Relaxed conversations and strong coffee with fragrant Finnish cardamom bread followed the inaugural speeches and tours, evoking once again the community spirit and the creative, sometimes contentious, energy that had drawn me in more than a half-century earlier.

Standing in Jinnee's refurbished, repurposed cottage, I recalled the lessons about awareness and imagination, solitude and sociability that had altered my viewpoints and my life. Jinnee's values—pragmatism, honesty, resilience—had helped me, in Robert Henri's words, to "blunder ahead" with composing a life of my own in the arts.

Beyond Jinnee's personal and artistic influence, I had also absorbed a deeper truth: there can be richness in the everyday, an "art spirit" in ordinary lives and ventures. The Folly Cove community exemplified for me the value of a local life—making things, harmonizing with nature, appreciating neighbors' gifts and tolerating quirks—and taking nothing for granted, because nothing lasts forever.

Life Stories Notes

***Your only salvation is in finding yourself…and you will never find yourself until you quit preconceiving what you will be when you have found* yourself:** Henri, *The Art Spirit*, page 195.

***Jinnee always came to terms*:** Cape Ann Museum (CAM) Folly Cove Designers Archive Collection A78, box #5, interviews by Professor Penny Martin: Interview with Aris Demetrios, San Francisco, CA, June 25, 1993.

***After the death of Carl Cherry*:** When Cherry passed away in 1947, leaving a sizeable fortune, Jeanne D'Orge founded the nonprofit Carl Cherry Center for the Arts to help support experimental fine arts and projects in the sciences.

***Can't tell you how sorry we are*:** Letter from VLB to Harold Burton, June 15, 1964.

***Harold, every so often*:** Letter from VLB to Harold Burton, August 23, 1964.

***Your call was one of the nicest*:** Letter from VLB to Selma and Harold Burton, September 9, 1964.

***Jinnee sent her annual*:** Christmas card from VLB to June Adler, December 17, 1965.

***Jinnee's sister Christine*:** Card with note from Christine Burton Braillard to Selma Burton, undated [1968].

Serge Nadejdin: A performer from St. Petersburg who had also directed films in Tsarist Russia. He immigrated to New York City after the Revolution. In 1932, Nadejdin was invited to take over the Russian Imperial Ballet School in Cleveland, Ohio. He directed the Nadejdin School of Ballet until his death in 1958.

The design sequence pictured: Each Folly Cove designer received a diploma after completing a successful first design. It depicts the stages in printmaking from idea to final product.

Art could become less remote: Choreographers forged ties with actors, poets, musicians, and artists. Dancer Merce Cunningham, composer John Cage, and visual artist Robert Rauschenberg and others collaborated on the early "Happenings." Painter Allen Kaprow declared in a 1966 essay that "the line between the Happening and daily life should be kept as fluid and perhaps indistinct as possible." For example, the Grand Union's unique group improvisations incorporated found objects, impromptu costuming, and random texts. Audiences could be included as part of performances. And Steve Paxton's contact improvisation duets in intimate studio settings explored the physics of movement for its own sake.

The Cape Ann Historical Association: *George Demetrios/ Sculptor and Teacher*, retrospective catalog, Cape Ann Historical Association, 1986.

By the fall of 2013: Our 2013 visit was a pilgrimage of sorts to mark the fifty-year anniversary of the summer of 1963.

Acknowledgments

Several people and institutions played a part in my writing process. Thanks go to my fellow Cumberland Street Writers for their sustaining support: Barbara Desmarais, Deb Gould, Judy Maloney, and Pam Smith. Also, special thanks to these insightful readers for helpful notes during many manuscript revisions: Linda Docherty, Deb Gould, Emmie Donadio, Christine Lundberg, and Susanna Natti.

Thanks to Cape Ann Museum Director Oliver Barker, Archivist/Librarian Trenton Carls, and Curatorial Assistant Leon Doucette for their generous assistance with the Virginia Lee Burton archives and Folly Cove Designer Collection. I'm obliged to Executive Director Robert Reese of the Carl Cherry Center for the Arts, Carmel, California, for making the Jeanne D'Orge archives available when my family and I visited. Thanks also to Clarion Books, an imprint of HarperCollins Publisher, LLC for permission to reprint images and text from Jinnee's books. I greatly appreciate photographer Michael Kolster's help with scanning the images.

Thanks to the many Cape Ann neighbors and friends I've named in this remembrance and also those I've not named who taught me meaningful lessons about human nature and community.

Closer to home, I am indebted to generations of our Burton family for saving mementos and correspondence that assisted me in shaping this personal memoir.

And closer still, loving thanks to my husband, David, exceptional editor and steadfast advocate.

About the Author

June Reading *ChooChoo* to Julien, 2021.
Photo credit Nick Vail.

J UNE ADLER VAIL FOUNDED BOWDOIN COLLEGE'S DANCE PROGRAM and, as professor, chaired the department of theater and dance, teaching courses in choreography and dance ethnography. Her previous books are *Cultural Choreographies* (1997) and *The Passion of Perfection: Gertrude Hitz Burton's Modern Victorian Life* (2017), Finalist, 2018 Maine Literary Award for Non-Fiction. She lives in Brunswick, Maine, with her husband, David, and enjoys reading with her grandchildren.

Visit her website at: www.junevail.com.

Permissions

Excerpt from *Mike Mulligan and his Steam Shovel* by Virginia Lee Burton. Copyright 1939 by Virginia Lee Burton, renewed 1967 by Virginia Lee Demetrios. Reprinted by permission of Clarion Books, an imprint of HarperCollins Publishers LLC.

Excerpt from *Katy and the Big Snow* by Virginia Lee Burton. Copyright 1943 by Virginia Lee Burton, renewed 1971 by George Demetrios. Reprinted by permission of Clarion Books, an imprint of HarperCollins Publishers LLC.

Excerpts from *Calico the Wonder Horse* by Virginia Lee Burton. Copyright 1941 by Virginia Lee Demetrios, renewed 1969 by Aristides Burton Demetrios and Michael Burton Demetrios. Reprinted by permission of Clarion Books, an imprint of HarperCollins Publishers LLC.

Excerpt from *ChooChoo* by Virginia Lee Burton. Copyright 1937 by Virginia Lee Burton, renewed 1964 by Aristides Burton Demetrios and Michael Burton Demetrios. Reprinted by permission of Clarion Books, an imprint of HarperCollins Publishers LLC.

Excerpt from *The Little House* by Virginia Lee Burton. Copyright 1942 by Virginia Lee Burton, renewed 1969 by Aristides Burton Demetrios and Michael Burton Demetrios. Reprinted by permission of Clarion Books, an imprint of HarperCollins Publishers LLC.

Excerpts from *Life Story* by Virginia Lee Burton. Copyright 1962 by Virginia Lee Demetrios, renewed 1990 by Aristides Burton Demetrios and Michael Burton Demetrios. Reprinted by permission of Clarion Books, an imprint of HarperCollins Publishers LLC.